# THE MEAL THAT HEALS

## PERRY STONE

Charisma
HOUSE
A STRANG COMPANY

Most STRANG COMMUNICATIONS/CHARISMA HOUSE/CHRISTIAN LIFE/EXCEL BOOKS/
FRONTLINE/REALMS/SILOAM products are available at special quantity discounts for bulk purchase for sales promotions, premiums, fund-raising, and educational needs. For details, write Strang
Communications/Charisma House/Christian Life/Excel Books/FrontLine/Realms/Siloam,
600 Rinehart Road, Lake Mary, Florida 32746, or telephone (407) 333-0600.

THE MEAL THAT HEALS by Perry Stone
Published by Charisma House
A Strang Company
600 Rinehart Road
Lake Mary, Florida 32746
www.charismahouse.com

Unless otherwise noted, all Scripture quotations are from the King James Version of the Bible.

Scripture quotations marked AMP are from the Amplified Bible. Old Testament copyright © 1965, 1987
by the Zondervan Corporation. The Amplified New Testament copyright © 1954, 1958, 1987 by the
Lockman Foundation. Used by permission.

Scripture quotations marked ASV are from the American Standard Bible.

Scripture quotations marked NIV are from the Holy Bible, New International Version.
Copyright © 1973, 1978, 1984, International Bible Society. Used by permission.

Scripture quotations marked NKJV are from the New King James Version of the Bible.
Copyright © 1979, 1980, 1982 by Thomas Nelson, Inc., publishers. Used by permission.

Design Director: Bill Johnson
Cover Designer: Jerry Pomales

Library of Congress Cataloging-in-Publication Data:
Stone, Perry F.
Meal that heals / Perry Stone. -- 1st ed.
    p. cm.
Includes bibliographical references (p.   ).
ISBN 978-1-59979-397-9
1. Lord's Supper. 2. Healing--Religious aspects--Christianity. 3.
Spiritual healing. I. Title.
BV825.3.S76 2008
234'.163--dc22
                                                                2008025487

First Edition

08 09 10 11 12 — 9 8 7 6 5 4 3 2 1
Printed in the United States of America

# DEDICATION

SEVERAL YEARS AGO I hosted a special friend, Dr. John Miller, on my weekly *Manna-fest* television program. Dr. Miller shared the concept of receiving Communion on a daily basis and how this important spiritual act was practiced daily from house to house in the early church. However, the practice was lost through centuries of tradition.

I am grateful for Dr. Miller's insight and inspiration on this subject, and I wish to give him honor as the man who helped me understand the importance of Communion and the blessings acquired by receiving the "meal that heals" every day.

# CONTENTS

*166*

# FOREWORD

CHERISE AND I HAVE had a friendship with Perry and Pam for more than twenty years. I have always been amazed at the insight and revelation that Perry has from God's Word. The extensiveness of his studies makes him a reliable source.

*The Meal That Heals* is the best book I have ever read on the subject of Communion. I highly recommend it to the person who wants a greater understanding of the Jewish culture and customs that impact the meaning of this important practice. As you read each chapter, the Scriptures will come alive and give you a renewed appreciation of Jesus's teaching and mandate to partake of the cup and the bread on a consistent basis.

Leviticus 17:11 declares, "The life of the flesh is in the blood." In other words, when blood is separated from flesh, death comes. On the cross Jesus's blood was separated from His flesh, resulting in His death. But in the Communion meal, Jesus's blood and flesh are reunited. If separating the blood from the body brought death, then reuniting the blood with the body of Christ through Communion brings life. Partaking of Communion gives life to your marriage, your church, and your physical body. It really is the meal that heals.

—JENTEZEN FRANKLIN
*New York Times* best-selling author of *Fasting*

PREFACE

THROUGHOUT CHURCH HISTORY, early truths that were once believed and practiced by first- and second-century believers were gradually removed or replaced by the traditions of religious leaders. For example, the love feast, a dinner that the rich prepared for the poor, was eventually stopped. So was the powerful early church practice of receiving the Lord's Supper (Communion) from house to house every day.

As the church age progressed, lost truths were revived. For example, the fifteenth century brought a revival of the doctrine of justification by faith. The Wesley brothers are credited with reviving the teaching of sanctification and a life of holiness. The early full gospel believers revived the doctrine of the infilling of the Holy Spirit and the gifts of the Spirit. And in the late 1940s, the teaching of divine healing as provided through the stripes that Christ bore was brought to the forefront.

Recently, the importance of fasting—a practice that marked the first-century believers—has been reemphasized, and millions of Christians have been encouraged to return to a powerful, biblical practice that brought spiritual results to the original New Testament church. Now, another lost practice is being revived—that of receiving Communion in your home—both for personal intimacy with Christ and to receive healing for your body, mind, and spirit.

I believe this book will open your understanding to a greater dimension of the new covenant and the healing power of Christ that manifests through the Lord's Supper, also called the Communion meal. It is my prayer that this powerful teaching will spread throughout the world and reform our traditional ideas as we return to spiritual concepts that have been lost through the ages. This book will explain the background of God's healing covenant and the importance of the blood and body of Christ. It will explain how Communion was established as a powerful tool to release the flow of God's healing power into every part of your being.

# INTRODUCTION

WHEN DID YOU LAST sit in a church service and receive the Lord's Supper? If you are Catholic, you receive the Communion meal at Mass on a weekly basis. If you are Protestant, you might receive the Lord's Supper, or Communion, once a month or as infrequently as once a year. Some churches have forgotten the power and importance of Communion, and the Communion bread has become stale and the grape juice has long fermented.

As a fourth-generation minister who was raised in a Christian church, I am very familiar with Communion. Growing up, I understood that Communion was administered only by a licensed or ordained minister in our denomination and received once a month or perhaps several times each year as the pastor determined. When Dr. John Miller first explained to me that Communion could be received every day, in a person's home, I was not certain there was enough biblical and historical information to confirm this.

After listening to him, I set out to personally research the idea of receiving Communion at home for both intimate fellowship with the Lord and for healing. The more I researched and discovered the various biblical nuggets, the more convinced I became that not only was it biblical, but it was also practiced daily from house to house by first-century Christians. It appears that man-made traditions and church authorities eventually stopped the practice as a Roman-style church system developed throughout the Mediterranean area from the third to fifth centuries.

Research resulted in a book called *The Meal That Heals*, which was printed several years ago. This book you are holding is a revised edition that contains even more information and insight to help the reader understand the revelation of Communion and the power of the blood and body of Christ.

We know that if Christ tarries for many more years, we will eventually depart this life. Hebrews 9:27 tells us that it is appointed for men to die once, but after this the judgment. However, Ecclesiastes 7:17 reveals that it is possible to die before our time. We must not depart this life before our appointed time, and we should desire to fulfill God's appointed destiny in this life. Since sickness and disease are in the earth, then understanding the healing power of the atoning work of Christ that is linked to the Communion meal could become a golden key that unlocks God's healing room.

I believe, just as the Bible tells us in Psalm 91:16, that it is God's will to satisfy us with long life and to show us His salvation. As you study this book, soak in the revelation of the Word and allow the Holy Spirit to speak to you. Then, in faith, put into action what you learn. God bless and keep you is my prayer!

# CHAPTER I

# GOD'S COVENANT OF HEALING FOR HIS CHILDREN

Bless the LORD, O my soul, and forget not all his benefits: Who forgiveth all thine iniquities; who healeth all thy diseases.

—PSALM 103:2–3

WHAT COMES TO MIND when I ask, "Are you saved?" To most Christians, salvation means the gift of eternal life through Jesus Christ after confessing and repenting of sins. Salvation is the key to entering heaven. In the New Testament, however, the word *saved* has a broader meaning. The Greek word for saved is *sozo*, and it is used fifty-seven times in the English translation of the Bible. In all but five references it is the same Greek word. According to *Strong's Concordance*, the word *sozo* means, "to save, deliver, protect, and heal."[1] Thus, salvation is a complete work of making a person whole in spirit, soul, and body.

When Christ healed the sick during His ministry, the Bible declared that they were made whole. In Matthew 9:21, the women with the issue of blood touched the border of Christ's garment and was made whole. When her faith touched Christ and she was healed, "[Jesus] said, Daughter . . . thy faith hath made thee whole. And the woman was whole from that hour" (v. 22). Three times in this narrative, the word *whole* is used. The Greek word for "whole" in these references is also *sozo*, the same word that is translated as "saved" throughout the New Testament.

Most Christian churches interpret *saved* as having your sins forgiven. God's Word, however, makes no theological distinction between the sin sickness of the spirit and sickness of the physical body as the traditional church does. Psalm 103:3 tells us that God forgives all of our iniquities and heals all of our diseases. God's will is for believers to be made whole and to walk in wholeness and blessing during their lifetimes. The most common New Testament word translated as "whole" (such as in 1 Thessalonians 5:23) is *holos,* which means "altogether."[2] To be completely whole, a person's body, soul, and spirit must function in peace and unity, without the disruption of sin in the spirit, sickness in the body, or depression and oppression in the mind.

## GOD'S UNIQUE HEALING COVENANT

When God first established His covenant with man, He also became man's great provider. This included provision of spiritual, financial, emotional, and physical needs—even physical healing. The first biblical reference to healing was when Abraham, God's covenant man, prayed for King Abimelech and his wife to have children. After the prayer, the king's wife gave birth, as we read in Genesis 20:17. The next reference to God's healing power is found in Exodus 15:26, where God made a healing covenant with the entire Hebrew nation after they come out of Egypt:

> And said, If thou wilt diligently hearken to the voice of the LORD thy God, and wilt do that which is right in his sight, and wilt give ear to his commandments, and keep all his statutes, I will put none of these diseases upon thee, which I have brought upon the Egyptians: for I am the LORD that healeth thee.
>
> —EXODUS 15:26

God announced that He is the Lord that heals. Throughout the Old Testament there are several compound names for God—that is, a Hebrew name that combines two Hebraic words that reveal a particular nature of God's character. Here are six of those Hebrew names:

| Hebrew Name | English Meaning | Biblical Reference |
|---|---|---|
| Jehovah-Jireh | God will provide it | Genesis 22:14 |
| Jehovah-Shalom | God our peace | Judges 6:24 |
| Jehovah-Tsidkeenu | God our righteousness | Jeremiah 23:6 |
| Jehovah-Sabaoth | God of hosts | 1 Samuel 1:3 |
| Jehovah-Shammah | God is present | Ezekiel 48:35 |
| Jehovah-Elyon | God most high | Psalm 7:17 |

Throughout the Old Testament, there are eight different Hebrew forms of words used for "heal" or "health." They mean, "to prolong life, to bind a wound, to heal all types of diseases."

In Exodus 15:26, God introduced Himself as Israel's healer and called Himself *Jehovah Rapha!* The Hebrew word *rapha* alludes to stitching something that has been torn, or completely repairing something that needs mended. Figuratively, it means to cure someone. This is more than just another Hebrew name for God. He was making a healing covenant for His people as they came out of Egypt toward the Promised Land. In Egypt there were many diseases and sicknesses that could spread like a plague throughout the population. God knew the Hebrews needed supernatural protection from these diseases and other sicknesses they might encounter among the various tribes living and passing through the Promised Land. Through His healing covenant God declared, "If you will obey My Word and walk in My commandments, I will prevent disease from coming upon you."

When Israel came out of Egyptian bondage, the Bible declares in Psalm 105:37, "He [God] brought them forth also with silver and gold: and there was not one feeble person among their tribes." Imagine six hundred thousand men, not counting the women and children, who marched across the Red Sea, healed and strengthened for the journey. God kept His promise! Weeks later, however, we read in Exodus 32:8 that these former Hebrews slaves broke God's instructions by worshiping a golden calf and giving their new idol credit for their deliverance from bondage. After weeks in the wilderness, this mixed multitude sinned by complaining against Moses and against God's plan for their deliverance. As a result, Numbers 21:6 records that fiery serpents and plagues were released among the people. It was not God's will that His chosen people experience such attacks. However, their willful disobedience blew a crack in the wall of God's protective hedge.

From the Exodus forward, the Old Testament reveals occasions where God demonstrated His healing and delivering power. Just a few examples are:

+ Miriam was healed of leprosy through Moses's prayers (Num. 12:13–15).
+ Naaman the Syrian was healed as he dipped in the Jordan River (2 Kings 5).
+ King Hezekiah was healed as he prayed to God (2 Kings 20).

In the last book of the Old Testament, Malachi released a prophecy about the future healing power of God that would arise through the "Sun of righteousness," a term used to identify the future Messiah of Israel:

> But unto you that fear my name shall the Sun of righteousness arise with healing in his wings; and ye shall go forth, and grow up as calves of the stall.
> —Malachi 4:2

The Messiah would bring spiritual light into the world in the same manner that the sun illuminates the earth. The phrase "healing in his wings" speaks of Messiah bringing healing to the nations. The Hebrew word for wings is *kanaph* and can refer to an edge of a garment.[3] This is the imagery of the Jewish prayer shawl that has fringes of threads draping from the bottom. The prayer shawl is worn at the synagogue, during prayer gatherings, and during special religious occasions. As a Jew, Christ would have worn this type of garment, and it was the hem of the garment—the fringes of threads—that the woman with the issue of blood touched and was made whole.

When she touched the hem of the garment of the "Sun of righteousness," she helped fulfill a prophecy that was written by Malachi four hundred year earlier!

By faith this woman pulled the long tassel on the corner of Christ's prayer shawl, and her faith pulled the healing anointing from Christ's body into her body. Christ said that virtue went out of His body:

> And Jesus, immediately knowing in himself that virtue had gone out of him, turned him about in the press…
>
> —MARK 5:30

In this verse, the English word *virtue* is the Greek word *dunamis,* which means, "miraculous power and ability."[4] This is important when we consider what Christ told believers would occur after they received the infilling of the Holy Spirit:

> But ye shall receive power, after that the Holy Ghost is come upon you…
>
> —ACTS 1:8

The word *power* in this verse is the same Greek word for "virtue" in Mark 5:30. The same power that was in the body of Christ is the same power that will come upon those who receive the Holy Spirit. This is how the apostles and the early church believers were able to carry on the healing ministry of Christ: through the ability given them by the power of the Holy Spirit.

## THE HEALING COVENANT IN THE NEW TESTAMENT

From Numbers 4:3 we learn that, in the ancient Jewish temple, a man could not enter the active priesthood until he was thirty years of age. Luke 3:23 tells us that Christ began His public ministry at about thirty years of age. In the time of the temple, when a diseased person believed they were healed, they were instructed to show themselves to the high priest, who was trained to examine the person to determine if the healing had actually occurred. On occasions, Christ instructed a healed person to confirm the miracle by showing himself to the high priest.

Under the old covenant, the healing name Jehovah-Rapha was revealed to the

Hebrew nation. In the time of Christ, He instructed His followers to ask the heavenly Father in His name, and He would do it (John 16:23). As the sick and diseased were brought to Christ, He ministered four levels of healing as revealed in the four Gospels:

1. Miracles of physical healing: Matthew 8:16
2. Miracles of casting out spirits: Mark 1:34
3. Creative miracles: Luke 22:51
4. Special miracles: John 2:3–10

Christ's miracles included healing the sick and diseased, opening the eyes of the blind and the ears of the deaf, causing those unable to talk to speak again, cleansing the lepers, raising the dead, and a host of countless miracles, so numerous that they all cannot be recorded in Scripture, according to John 21:25. There were creative miracles that involved turning water into wine, multiplying bread and fish, and restoring an ear that had been severed from a man's head.

Not only did Christ perform miracles, but He also commissioned His own disciples to go forth preaching the kingdom of God and healing the sick in every city where they ministered:

> Then he called his twelve disciples together, and gave them power and authority over all devils, and to cure diseases. And he sent them to preach the kingdom of God, and to heal the sick.
>
> —LUKE 9:1–2

Christ later appointed seventy men to go out in teams of two, preaching, healing the sick, and casting out evil spirits. Luke records the spiritual success these men had in their ministry:

> And the seventy returned again with joy, saying, Lord, even the devils are subject unto us through thy name.
>
> —LUKE 10:17

Throughout Christ's ministry, He not only gave a message of hope and salvation, but He also combined the message of eternal salvation with healing of the mind and body. The physical healing was the drawing card to bring multitudes to Christ who would preach the message of the kingdom of God, and then demonstrate the power of the kingdom by delivering the oppressed and the sick.

Today, some ministers teach that the healing anointing was transferred from Christ only to the original twelve apostles to assist in the birth of the church and the spread of Christianity. This cannot be true because, throughout the Book of Acts, men who were not apostles ministered healing to the sick. Such was the case when a deacon named Ananias laid his hands upon Saul of Tarsus and he was instantly healed of blindness (Acts 9:12–18). Phillip was not one of the original twelve apostles, but he preached and witnessed miracles of healing with people being delivered from evil spirits as he ministered in the city of Samaria. James wrote that the elders of the church could anoint the sick with oil and pray the prayer of faith over them, and God would heal the afflicted person (James 5:14). It is religious theological tradition—not the Bible—that limits God's healing covenant to a certain period in church history.

## Healing in Church History

The idea that certain gifts of healing ceased after the death of John, the last apostle, is commonly taught from pulpits in certain churches throughout North America. This theory is a man-made interpretation based on ideas of liberal theologians and is not in agreement with true church history. The early fathers and bishops of the first centuries wrote about the continuation of miracles manifesting among believers in the church.

> For numberless demoniacs throughout the world and in your city, many of our Christian men exorcizing them in the name of Jesus Christ, who was crucified under Pontius Pilate, have healed, and do heal rendering helpless

and driving the possessing devils out of men, though they could not be cured
by all the other exorcists and those who used incantations and drugs.[5]

—JUSTIN MARTYR, A.D. 165

Those who are in truth His disciples, receiving grace from Him, do in His
name perform miracles…and truly drive out devils.…Others still, heal the
sick by laying their hands upon them and they are made whole. Yea, more-
over, as I have said, the dead have even been raised up, and remained among
us for many years.[6]

—IRENAEUS, A.D. 200

And some give evidence of having received through their faith a marvellous power by the cures which they perform, revoking no other name over
those who need their help than that of the God of all things, and of Jesus,
along with a mention of His history. For by these means we too have seen
many persons freed from grievous calamities, and…other ills, which could
be cured neither by men or devils.[7]

—ORIGEN, A.D. 250

Clement mentions in A.D. 275 that there were "men who have received the gift
of healing from God, confidently, to the glory of God."[8]

In A.D. 429, Theodore of Mopsueste said, "Many heathen amongst us are being
healed by Christians from whatsoever sickness they have, so abundant are the miracles in our midst."[8]

Healings and miracles began with Abraham and continued through the New
Testament and into the first several centuries of the church, because healing is a
part of God's name, His nature, and His covenant. We still can have miracles today
because Hebrews 13:8 says that Jesus is the same yesterday, today, and forever.

## HEALING IS A COVENANT

There is no such thing as a day of miracles or a day of healing; there is only a covenant
of healing established by God. This covenant of healing can be manifested through
several different methods of healing found in the Bible. According to Dr. John Miller,

there were nineteen people recorded in the four Gospels who were delivered through the ministry of Jesus. Of the nineteen, there were eleven whose problem was caused by a spirit. Others received healing from diseases that afflicted their bodies.

There are four avenues in which miracles can operate:

1. Miracles can happen through signs and wonders: Hebrews 2:4.
2. Miracles can happen because of an anointing: Acts 10:38.
3. Miracles can happen through deliverance: Luke 4:18.
4. Miracles can happen through faith in the atonement: 1 Peter 2:24.

Using Scripture as our guide, there are six New Testament (covenant) methods used to provide healing. While there are many scriptures to back up each method, I will list only one reference. Healing can manifest through:

1. Laying hands on the sick: Mark 16:18
2. Anointing the sick with oil and praying in faith: James 5:14–15
3. Gifts of healing and miracles: 1 Corinthians 12:7–10
4. The spoken word: Psalm 107:20
5. An act of obedience: John 9:6–7
6. Receiving Communion: 1 Corinthians 11:25–31

After hearing many messages throughout the years on Christ's healing power, I was familiar with the first five methods listed above. However, along with most believers, I never heard a message preached on the Communion meal and its link to healing. Since the great healing revival in the 1940s, the laying on of hands and anointing with oil have been the most common methods of asking God for healing. However, it is time to understand the potential power of the Lord's Supper. After all, the Lord's Supper is part of the covenant of healing.

## For Your Reflection

1. Why was it important for God to establish a healing covenant with the Israelites at the time they began their journey out of the bondage of Egypt and toward the Promised Land?

_____

_____

2. What is the symbolism of the verse in Malachi 4:2, which says, "The Sun of righteousness [shall] arise with healing in his wings…"?

_____

_____

3. What evidence does the Book of Acts give to refute the belief of some people that the power to heal was made available only to the original twelve apostles?

_____

_____

4. List the six New Testaments methods used to heal the sick.

   a. Mark 16:18

_____

   b. James 5:14–15

_____

   c. 1 Corinthians 12:7–10

_____

   d. Psalm 107:20

_____

   e. John 9:6–7

_____

   f. 1 Corinthians 11:25–31

_____

# CHAPTER 2

# UNDERSTANDING THE COMMUNION MEAL

The cup of blessing which we bless, is it not the communion of the blood of Christ? The bread which we break, is it not the communion of the body of Christ?

—1 CORINTHIANS 10:16

WHAT DOES IT MEAN when we speak of receiving Communion? Most Christians identify this as a sacred time set aside under the leadership of ministers in the church when believers receive the bread and the fruit of the vine as a reminder of Christ's finished work on the cross. For many Christians this is celebrated once a week, once a month, or once a year. The bread and the fruit of the vine (the juice) are called the sacrament. The classical Latin word *sacrament* referred to the oath a soldier took to be faithful to his commander. The religious term is accredited to Pliny's letter to Trajan (c. 112) when he wrote that Christians "bind themselves by an oath [*sacramento*], not for the commission of some crime, but to avoid acts of theft, brigandage, and adultery, not to break their word, and not to withhold money deposited with them when asked for it."[1] The Protestants have two sacraments (baptism and Communion), while the Catholics and Greek Orthodox add to this list confirmation, penance, extreme unction, ordination, and matrimony.

The Catholics participate in Mass in which the priest offers the bread and wine called the Eucharist. The word *Eucharist* comes from ancient Greek, and it means "to give thanks" or "thanksgiving." The word is found in the Greek New Testament in Matthew 15:36, Mark 8:6, Mark 14:23, and other places. In the above cases Jesus gave thanks. Today, we give thanks by saying grace at the dinner table. Thus, the Eucharist is the blessing of the elements of Communion. During the Eucharist, Catholics believe the bread becomes the literal body of Christ and the wine becomes the literal blood of Christ. This teaching is called "transubstantiation." Catholics say that in Mass, the same sacrifice that Jesus offered on the cross is offered again. This doctrine states that somehow the bread and the fruit of the vine are miraculously converted into the literal body and blood of Jesus when blessed by the priest before it is administered.

Transubstantiation is the belief that:

> …at the moment of Consecration [by a priest or church official] … the elements [of bread and wine] are not only spiritually transformed, but rather are actually (substantially) transformed into the Body and Blood of Christ. The elements retain the appearance … of bread and wine, but are indeed the actual Body and Blood of Christ.… Christ is truly and substantially present in the Eucharist.[2]

This view says that while the bread still looks, feels, smells, and taste like bread, it literally becomes the flesh of Jesus. Thus, everyone who eats the bread of Communion eats Jesus's flesh, weather he eats it in faith or in unbelief. The difficulty of this view is that it places Jesus's body and blood here on Earth every time someone celebrates the Lord's Supper.

Consider this fact. Right now Jesus is literally in heaven at the right hand of the Father (Acts 7:55; Eph. 1:20; Col. 3:1; Heb. 8:1). He will return in bodily form at the rapture, and we will see Him just as He is. On the other hand, the Lutherans believe in a doctrine called "consubstantiation." This means that in Communion, the blood and body of Christ and the bread and the wine coexist with each other.[3] They believe that the fundamental substance of the body and the blood of Christ is present alongside the bread and the cup.

Some of the confusion as to interpretation comes from a statement that Jesus made in John 6:53: "Most assuredly, I say to you, unless you eat the flesh of the Son of Man and drink His blood, you have no life in you" (NKJV).

Consubstantiation is the view that the bread and the cup of Communion coexist and are equal to the flesh and blood of Jesus, but still remain the bread and the wine. Transubstantiation is the view that the bread and the wine become the actual body and blood of Jesus.

I believe the following view is the correct view. After Jesus took the bread and the fruit of the vine, He gave these elements to the disciples and said, "This is my body…this is my blood" (Matt. 26:26–28). He was not speaking literally because He was seated with them in a literal body holding the cup and bread in His physical hands. Jesus specifically identified the drink in the cup as fruit of the vine in verse 29. Therefore the physical nature of the elements of the supper had not changed.

It is clear that Christ was representing His body and blood by comparing them to the bread and the fruit of the vine of Communion. Jesus often spoke in metaphors, a figure of speech that represents that very thing. Jesus called Himself the vine in John 15:5, but He did not mean that He was a piece of vegetation. In John 10:9 He said, "I am the door," but He was not saying that He would turn Himself into a piece of wood.

Another point is that when Christ said, "This [Communion] do in remembrance of me" (Luke 22:19), it is a memorial of His accomplished work. If He literally became the bread and body, then it would no longer be in remembrance. In Matthew 26:26–28, when Jesus was holding the cup and the bread and stating this was the blood of the new covenant, if He was turning the elements into His literal body, then He was in His body while holding another body in His hand. Although Christ had the nature of God and man, He was not in two separate bodies.

In the nineteenth century, Bishop J. C. Ryle wrote in *Light From Old Times* that if you believe the bread and cup become the actual body and blood of Christ in the partaking of Communion, you are denying three things:

1.  You are denying Christ's finished work on the cross. Jesus cried, "It is finished." A sacrifice that needs to be repeated is neither a perfect nor a complete sacrifice.

2.  You are denying the priestly office of Christ. If the Communion elements were His literal body and blood, then the elements themselves would become the sacrifice for sins. For anyone besides Christ to offer our Lord's body and blood to God as a sacrifice of sin is to rob our heavenly High Priest of His glory.

3.  You are denying Christ's human nature. If His literal body can be in more than one place at the same time, then He did not have a body like ours, and Jesus was not the last Adam in that He did not have our nature.[4]

If a person accepts the teaching of transubstantiation, then it is understandable there is a fear in handling the bread and wine because of the belief that it becomes the literal body and blood of Jesus. Thus the power of a human earthly priesthood in the church becomes necessary to give the Communion. If, however, the actual meaning is that the bread and wine *represent* the body and blood of the Savior, then we can accept that an individual believer in covenant with Christ already has direct access to come boldly before Christ's throne at this moment. And because of this personal relationship, the believer has the wonderful honor of fellowshiping with the Lord through the Communion meal.

Among both Protestant and Catholic groups, importance is placed on the bread and the juice (or wine). The primary difference is the Protestants believe the bread and wine represent the body and blood of Christ, while the Catholics believe the bread and wine become the literal body and blood of Christ.

In Scripture, the word *Communion* is used in three verses (twice in 1 Corinthians 10:16; 2 Corinthians 6:14; and 2 Corinthians 13:14). Twice it alludes to the Lord's Supper. Communion comes from a Greek word *koinonia*, which means intimate partnership or intercourse.[5] It is a very personal and intimate word.

## How Did Communion Originate?

The first mention of the use of bread and wine is when Abraham went to Jerusalem and met Melchizedek, the first king and priest of the Most High God. The man Melchizedek is a mysterious figure whom Christian theology teaches was a preview of Christ; Jewish teachers say he was Shem, the son of Noah, through whom the linage of the future Messiah would come.

In Genesis 14, Abraham traveled to Jerusalem (called Salem at that time, according to Genesis 14:18), and there, in a valley that would later be called the Kidron Valley, Abraham met a priest whose name, Melchizedek, consists of two Hebrew words: Melech (king) and Zadok (righteousness). This man served in the combined position of both a king and priest. This king of Jerusalem brought forth bread and wine and pronounced a special blessing upon Abraham.

> And Melchizedek king of Salem brought forth bread and wine: and he was the priest of the most high God. And he blessed him, and said, Blessed be Abram of the most high God, possessor of heaven and earth.
>
> —Genesis 14:18–19

This act was significant for several reasons. First, this area of Jerusalem was marked at that moment as God confirmed His covenant with Abraham, sealing the covenant with the bread and the wine. Second, years later, God required that Abraham return to the Land of Moriah to offer his son Isaac on an altar (Gen. 22:2). The land of Moriah was the same area where Abraham and Melchizedek had met and communed. A third point is that while Abraham was offering Isaac on Mount Moriah, he predicted that one day God would provide Himself a lamb, and Abraham predicted that in that very location (the mountain of the Lord) it (the lamb) would be seen!

> And Isaac spake unto Abraham his father, and said, My father: and he said, Here am I, my son. And he said, Behold the fire and the wood: but where is the lamb for a burnt offering? And Abraham said, My son, God will provide himself a lamb for a burnt offering: so they went both of them together.
>
> —Genesis 22:7–8

And Abraham called the name of that place Jehovah-jireh: as it is said to this day, In the mount of the LORD it shall be seen.

—GENESIS 22:14

Two thousand years later Christ, the Lamb of God, appeared in Jerusalem and offered Himself as the final sacrifice on the cross, near the same mountain where Abraham went to offer Isaac. Prior to His death, Christ offered the bread and the cup to His disciples, announcing a new covenant. This Last Supper, as it is commonly called, was being celebrated before the Jewish Passover. The Jewish Passover was the perfect picture of the in-depth meaning of the power of the blood and body of Christ.

## THE FIRST PASSOVER

Over thirty-five hundred years ago the Hebrew nation had become slaves to the Egyptians. Pharaoh, the king of Egypt, was unwilling to release the Hebrews and allow them to return to Israel. God sent ten plagues among the Egyptians. The final plague led to the freedom of the Hebrews and the deaths of the Egyptian firstborn.

The tenth plague involved the death angel moving from house to house, taking the life of the firstborn, both men and beasts (Exod. 11:5). To protect the Hebrews from the destroying angel, God required each Hebrew house to place the blood of a lamb on the left, right, and top post of the door, and then eat all of the lamb before midnight (Exod. 12:7–8). The miracle was twofold. By eating the lamb, the Hebrews experienced supernatural healing, as indicated in Scripture:

He brought them forth also with silver and gold: and there was not one feeble person among their tribes.

—PSALM 105:37

The other miracle was that the destroying angel was restrained from entering homes freshly marked with lamb's blood on the doorpost. Thus the Hebrew families were protected from both sickness and death as a result of the blood and the body of the lamb. God said their obedience of marking the door with lamb's blood would cause the death angel to pass over their house:

And the blood shall be to you for a token upon the houses where ye are: and
when I see the blood, I will pass over you, and the plague shall not be upon
you to destroy you, when I smite the land of Egypt.

—Exodus 12:13

God instructed the Hebrews to make this event a yearly memorial forever, celebrated each year on the fourteenth day of the first month. The entire nation of
Israel was to celebrate Passover, reminding future generations of how God brought
Israel out of Egypt with mighty signs and wonders (Lev. 23:5). The Hebrew word
for Passover is *Pesach,* and it means to skip over, to leap, or to dance. The word
indicates how God demanded the angel of death to skip over the homes of the
Hebrews, which were protected by the lamb's blood. Each year religious Jews
conduct a Passover *seder* in which they tell the story of deliverance from Egypt.
During this season all leaven must be removed from the house for seven days
(Exod. 12:15–19). Also, four different cups of wine are used, with each cup identifying a different aspect of the Passover story. The cups are numbered and named
in the following order:

- The first is the cup of sanctification.
- The second is the cup of affliction.
- The third is the cup of redemption.
- The fourth is the cup of consummation, or hallel.

For centuries, religious Jews have commemorated the departure of their ancestors from Egypt by conducting a yearly Passover in the home. The first revelation of the blood and body of the lamb transpired in Egypt in the homes of the
Hebrews, and centuries later we see the supper enacted in an upper room with
Christ and His chosen disciples.

## The Lord's Supper

Prior to His trial and crucifixion, Christ met in a large room with His disciples.
That evening Christ made an announcement. Since four cups are used at the

Passover table and each cup is named, most scholars believe that as Christ held up the third cup (the cup of redemption), He amazed His disciples by saying:

> Likewise also the cup after supper, saying, This cup is the new testament in my blood, which is shed for you.
>
> —LUKE 22:20

Christ was introducing a new covenant that would be sealed by His own blood. No longer would future Passovers among believers allude to freedom from Egypt, but believers would rejoice for their deliverance from sin, sickness, and the power of Satan! Just as religious Jews honor the ancient Passover each year and remember their night of redemption, each time a Christian lifts the cup to his lips and receives the bread of Communion, he is reminded of his past deliverance from the penalty of sin, his present deliverance from the power of sin, and his future redemption from the presence of sin!

## THE PROPHETIC FULFILLMENT OF PASSOVER

Christ's crucifixion was a perfect correlation of a prophetic fulfillment of the ancient Passover in Egypt. Pharaoh is a picture of Satan, who held us in captivity, and Egypt represents the bondages of the world system. The blood of the lamb in Egypt is a type and shadow of the precious blood of Jesus, who was identified as the Lamb of God (John 1:29). There were three marks of blood on the doorposts of the Hebrew home in Egypt, located on the left, right and top posts (Exod. 12:7). The correlation is that, at the time of Christ's crucifixion, there were three crosses with victims hanging on them; a thief on the left, one on the right, and Christ in the middle (Matt. 27:38).

Another parallel between the ancient patterns of redemption and the crucifixion is identified during an appointed season occurring each year called "Yom Kippur," or the Day of Atonement. On this sixth feast of Israel, the high priest brought two identical goats before him. He marked one for the Lord and the other for Azazel. The Lord's goat was slaughtered and burnt on the altar at the temple. Afterward, the priest laid hands on the head of the Azazel goat, transferring the sins of Israel onto this goat. Called the scapegoat, this goat was led by a priest with a rope into the wilderness and met its death when it was eventually pushed off a large rugged mountain ledge.

Another Day of Atonement tradition developed with three red threads. The priest tied one thread to the neck of the goat for the Lord and another to the neck of the scapegoat. A third thread was hung from the door of the temple in Jerusalem. Jewish tradition states that when the scapegoat died in the wilderness, the red thread on the temple door turned white, indicating that Israel's sins were now remitted and forgiven.[6] This is why Isaiah wrote:

> Though your sins be as scarlet, they shall be white as snow; though they be
> red like crimson, they shall be as wool.
> —ISAIAH 1:18

These three red threads correlate with the three men hanging on the three crosses on Golgotha. One man, Christ, was dying for the Lord. Another man, a bitter thief, died carrying his sin, like the scapegoat. A third man, another thief, changed his eternal destiny while hanging beside Jesus. His sins became white as snow in the same manner that the red thread turned white on the temple doors, indicating the remission of sins!

In the crucifixion story we can even see a correlation between the two identical goats, one that dies at the temple and one that is released in the wilderness, dying later. Christ is the sacrifice who died in Jerusalem, while a man named Barabbas was released by Pilate prior to the crucifixion (Matt. 27:16–22). The name *Barabbas* is interesting. *Bar* means "son," and *abbas* means "exalted father." Jesus was the Son of the true Father, and Barabbas had an exalted earthly father. The name of Jesus in Hebrew is Yeshuah, and according to one tradition, the actual first name of Barabbas was Yeshuah Barabbas. This indicates that both Christ and Barabbas had the same first names, just as both goats on the Day of Atonement were to be identical. The difference: Jesus died for the Lord and Barabbas escaped as a sinner.

Both Passover and the Day of Atonement depict the redemption of mankind through the suffering and resurrection of Christ! Religious Jews and Messianic believers celebrate Passover each spring as a reminder of God's mighty deliverance in bringing His people out of Egyptian slavery.

## BACK TO THE COMMUNION SUPPER

In the Christian church, believers recognize the historical application of Passover and see the prophetic fulfillment in Christ, who, as God's final Lamb, died during Passover (Matt. 26:19). Just as the Jewish Passover reminds the Hebrews of their great day of redemption from Egypt and their future promise of inheriting the Promised Land, so Communion is a reminder of our redemption through Christ's suffering and of our future inheritance with Christ in heaven!

During the first Passover, the flesh of a lamb was eaten at the table of the Hebrew family, and the lamb's flesh brought supernatural healing for the journey through the wilderness. The blood on the door stopped the destroying angel from taking the life of the Hebrew firstborn. Thus the body and the blood of the Passover lamb brought complete healing and redemption.

The body of Christ, God's final Lamb, brought healing through the wounds and stripes on His body and salvation through His blood on the cross. Communion is a sign of our belief in Christ's finished work and a testimony of our faith in the complete work of salvation.

How often should a believer receive Communion? How often did the first-century believers receive Communion? Part of the answer lies with understanding the New Testament term, breaking of bread.

## FOR YOUR REFLECTION

1.  In your own words, what is the difference between the Catholic belief in transubstantiation regarding Communion and the Protestant belief in consubstantiation regarding Communion?

    _____

    _____

    _____

2. Now state in your own words the explanation that the author believes is the correct understanding of Communion seen through Jesus's use of metaphors.

_____

_____

_____

3. Every year the Jews celebrate Passover. When did the first Passover happen, and what were the circumstances that caused it?

_____

_____

_____

4. Name the four cups used at the Passover.

    a. The cup of _____

    b. The cup of _____

    c. The cup of _____

    d. The cup of _____

5. What is the correlation between Communion and each of the following:

    a. The three marks of blood on the doorposts of the Hebrew homes in Egypt

_____

_____

_____

b.  The three red threads used by priests on the Day of Atonement

_____

_____

_____

c.  The flesh of the lamb eaten at the first Passover and the blood of
    the Passover lamb

_____

_____

_____

# CHAPTER 3

# What Does It Mean to Break Bread?

*And they, continuing daily with one accord in the temple, and breaking bread from house to house, did eat their meat with gladness and singleness of heart.*

—Acts 2:46

THIS BOOK EMPHASIZES RECEIVING daily Communion, especially when you need healing. Is there biblical precedent of early believers receiving Communion every day, or was it just during certain marked occasions? To understand the concept of receiving Communion every day, one must examine the Book of Acts and the historical records of the first-century Christians. Two passages found in the New Testament indicate that believers went from house to house breaking bread. What is the true meaning of this phrase, and how does it relate to daily Communion?

## The Breaking of Bread

There are two main references in the New Testament where we are told that Jesus broke bread.

*And as they were eating, Jesus took bread, and blessed it, and brake it, and gave it to the disciples, and said, Take, eat; this is my body*

—Matthew 26:26

At this event, called the Last Supper, Christ introduced the new covenant to His disciples. After His resurrection, Christ met with His disciples to again to break bread:

> And it came to pass, as he sat at meat with them, he took bread, and blessed it, and brake, and gave to them.
>
> —LUKE 24:30

At the Last Supper with His disciples, Christ mentioned the cup of consummation (fourth cup) (Matt. 26:27). The fourth cup of wine, however, is not mentioned after the resurrection account, only that Christ broke bread with them. Christ had already stated that He would not drink from the (fourth) cup again until He drank it anew in the kingdom:

> But I say unto you, I will not drink henceforth of this fruit of the vine, until that day when I drink it new with you in my Father's kingdom.
>
> —MATTHEW 26:29

The glorious promise of drinking the cup in the kingdom alludes to the future Marriage Supper of the Lamb, where the saints who have received and walked in the new covenant of Christ's blood will seal and consummate their marriage to the Lamb of God (Christ) at a wedding supper in heaven (Rev. 19:9).

Shortly after Christ's resurrection, He appeared to two men on the road to Emmaus. They were unaware it was Christ as He expounded the prophecies concerning the Messiah to them. Christ was invited into their home, and there He broke bread with them. Suddenly their eyes were opened and they knew Him (Luke 24:31). Then we read:

> And they told what things were done in the way, and how he was known of them in breaking of bread.
>
> —LUKE 24:35

This event initiated a continual custom or tradition among the first-century believers: breaking bread from house to house and celebrating the resurrection of

Christ and the promise that He would again return for them. This breaking of bread was a term used in the Bible to describe the fellowship of the Lord's Table or the Communion being practiced in the homes of believers.

## House-to-House References

The first converts to Christ were Jewish believers. The church was birthed on the Hebrew feast of Pentecost, and over three thousand Jewish converts were baptized in water (Acts 2:1–41). Shortly after this event, persecution broke out in Jerusalem, and eventually it became a physical risk for the Hebrew believers to worship at the temple (Acts 4:1–21; 5:17–40; 21:27–31). Before his conversion, Paul confessed to persecuting believers from city to city (Acts 26:11). As the Christian faith grew, so did the persecution. This persecution eventually led believers to worship in their own homes and the homes of fellow believers (Acts 5:42).

At the beginning of the Christian era, churches began in believers' homes, as this was a safer place to meet and worship without the threat from religious leaders of the synagogues or persecution from certain Pharisees, Sadducees, and priests at the temple. In their home groups believers would study, pray, and sing hymns (Eph. 5:19).

The Bible reveals several names of the believers whose homes became churches:

+ Aquila and Priscilla had a church in their house (Rom. 16:3, 5).
+ Nymphas at Laodicea had a church in his house (Col. 4:15).
+ Apphia and Archippus had a church in their house (Philem. 2).

Believers would also meet together on the first day of the week (Acts 20:7; 1 Cor. 16:2), during which time they would break bread. The first day of the week on the Jewish calendar is Sunday.

> And upon the first day of the week, when the disciples came together to break bread, Paul preached unto them, ready to depart on the morrow; and continued his speech until midnight.
>
> —Acts 20:7

Scripture indicates the practice of breaking of bread was a central part of the early activity among believers in their homes.

> And they, continuing daily with one accord in the temple, and breaking bread from house to house, did eat their meat with gladness and singleness of heart.
>
> —ACTS 2:46

> And day after day they regularly assembled in the temple with united purpose, and in their homes they broke bread [including the Lord's Supper]. They partook of their food with gladness and simplicity and generous hearts.
>
> —ACTS 2:46, AMP

While growing up in church, the Sunday evening services were considered more exciting and spiritual than the Sunday morning services. After the service, it was common for believers to go out and fellowship at a local restaurant. This is where we spent time talking about the Word and getting to know each other. We affectionately called it breaking bread.

For years when I read where the early church broke bread from house to house, I assumed it alluded to simply having a dinner in someone's house. Only after research did I understand the true meaning of this term and why this was an important daily activity for the early saints. According to numerous Christian commentaries, the daily breaking of bread referred to having the Lord's Supper (Communion) in the believer's house! Remember, the original Passover supper was in the homes of the Hebrews in Egypt, and the Lord's Supper was initially instituted by Christ from a home.

Below is a list of nine references that give commentary on Acts 2:42, Acts 20:7, and 1 Corinthians 10:16. They are commenting on the phrase, "breaking of bread from house to house."

> [Breaking of bread] The Syriac renders this "the eucharist" or the Lord's Supper.[1]
>
> —BARNES NOTES

[And in breaking of bread] Whether this means the holy eucharist, or their common meals, it is difficult to say. The Syriac understands it of the former. Breaking of bread was that act which preceded a feast or meal, and which, was performed by the master of the house, when he pronounced the blessing—what we would call grace before meat. See the form at Matt 26:26.[2]

—ADAM CLARKE'S COMMENTARY

And in breaking of bread. From Acts 20:7, 11, and 1 Cor. 10:16, it seems pretty certain that partaking of the Lord's Supper is what is here meant. But just as when the Lord's Supper was first instituted it was preceded by the full paschal meal, so a frugal repast seems for a considerable time to have preceded the Eucharistic feast.[3]

—JAMIESON, FAUSSET, AND BROWN COMMENTARY

They frequently joined in the ordinance of the Lord's supper. They continued in the breaking of bread, in celebrating that memorial of their Master's death, as those that were not ashamed to own their relation to, and their dependence upon, Christ and him crucified. They could not forget the death of Christ, yet they kept up this memorial of it, and made it their constant practice, because it was an institution of Christ, to be transmitted to the succeeding ages of the church. They broke bread from house to house; kat' oikon - house by house; they did not think fit to celebrate the eucharist in the temple, for that was peculiar to the Christian institutes, and therefore they administered that ordinance in private houses, choosing such houses of the converted Christians as were convenient, to which the neighbours resorted; and they went from one to another of these little synagogues or domestic chapels, houses that had churches in them, and there celebrated the eucharist with those that usually met there to worship God.[4]

—MATTHEW HENRY'S COMMENTARY

It is generally supposed that the early disciples attached so much significance to the breaking of bread at the ordinary meals, more than our saying
grace, that they followed the meal with the Lord's Supper.[5]

—WORD PICTURES IN THE NEW TESTAMENT

The breaking of bread, the administering and receiving of the Holy Communion, in the breaking of the Eucharist....The usage of the primitive
church was to have this daily.[6]

—THE BIBLE COMMENTARY

Celebrating the Lord's Supper. At first observed on the evening of every
day...who also continued in the temple praising God and celebrating the
Lord's Supper in their homes...[7]

—THE PREACHERS COMPLETE HOMILETIC COMMENTARY

They continued steadfastly in the breaking of bread, i.e., in celebrating the
Sacrament of Lord's Supper, or Holy Communion. At first the Lord's Supper was celebrated daily...[8]

—A COMMENTARY OF THE HOLY BIBLE

Breaking bread from house to house. They naturally observed their particular
Holy Rite, the Sacrament of the New Covenant, apart from the public...[9]

—LANGE'S COMMENTARY ON THE HOLY SCRIPTURES

These different Christian commentaries written by biblical scholars all agree
that the phrase "breaking of bread" refers to receiving Communion, the Eucharist,
or the Lord's Supper. All three terms identify the same sacred rite of receiving the
bread and fruit of the vine for the Communion meal. Again, notice this was originally done daily from house to house (Acts 2:46).

## AS OFTEN AS YOU DO THIS

From the time of the Exodus, the Jewish Passover was celebrated once a year on the
fourteenth of Nissan, which usually falls in the spring months of March or April.
Christ was crucified at the season of Passover and introduced the new covenant

during this season. Some Messianic believers teach that Communion should be received only once a year at Passover. However, the Bible says, "As oft as ye [do] it…" (1 Cor. 11:25), which does not regulate a certain timeframe or particular season. The Communion meal was so important among the early church that it was conducted every day from house to house. Perhaps this was to ensure that the many new believers scattered throughout a city would enjoy the personal and intimate fellowship with the Lord through His sacred meal among the faithful.

## THE LOVE FEASTS

The New Testament also speaks of the love (agape) feasts in Jude 12. The love feasts were hosted by wealthier members of the church who provided a special meal for the poor in their congregations. The love feasts included the poor, the widows, the orphans, and others who lacked funds for personal needs. Some scholars believe these were conducted every evening in connection with the Communion.[10] By the second century, the agape feast was separated from the Communion as two distinct rituals. The Communion was conducted at the conclusion of the morning service and the love feast later in the day.

According to early Christian history, these feasts continued in the church until the fourth century, when they were banned by the council of Laodicea. Some suggest that this action also caused the house-to-house Communion to be slowly deemphasized as believers began receiving it only in the local churches. While there is no direct reference among historians as to why the breaking of bread was moved from house to house to an activity solely conducted in the church facilities, it appears to be because as the church grew, buildings were constructed in communities where the believers met weekly in local churches instead of homes. Thus the local church became the heart of all spiritual activity instead of the homes of individual believers.

I personally suspect that the central religious system, which developed out of the Church of Rome, resisted allowing the common people to have any form of spiritual authority outside of the church hierarchy. Thus by initiating that the Lord's Supper (called the Mass, in Latin) could be performed only by a priest in the church, it motivated the believers to be faithful to the church and kept under the authority of the leadership.

While the Bible certainly teaches spiritual authority and subjection to those over you in the Lord (Heb. 13:7), the love feasts were forgotten and the Lord's Supper became more of a weekly spiritual ritual for some instead of a fellowship and healing meal in the quiet intimacy of a believer's home.

## WALKING IN HEALING IN THE BEGINNING

An important part of the Communion meal is the aspect of healing that is provided through Christ's atonement. During the earliest days of the church, it appears the believers walked in a realm of health, joy, and strength. However, as hidden sins, disobedience, unforgiveness, and strife entered the congregation and spread like cancer through the members of the body, some believers experienced weakness, became sick, or died prematurely. This is clear from Paul's letter to the church at Corinth:

> For he that eateth and drinketh unworthily, eateth and drinketh damnation to himself, not discerning the Lord's body. For this cause many are weak and sickly among you, and many sleep.
> —1 CORINTHIANS 11:29–30

The early church "had all things common" (Acts 4:32). As long as the believers walked in love (remember the love feasts), centered their message on Christ, and maintained a life of forgiveness and holiness, they fulfilled the days of their life, growing in God's grace. The major satanic attack the early believers experienced was persecution, which is guaranteed for those who live by the Word of God (Mark 4:17). Then and today, strife and envy in the church breed confusion and every evil work (James 3:16). This evil work unlocks a door for the enemy to enter as the person gives place to the devil (Eph. 4:27).

## THE CHURCH AT CORINTH

Some in the church at Corinth were opening this door to the devil. Paul wrote two separate, detailed letters to this church: First and Second Corinthians. He began his first letter exposing the fact that the believers were experiencing contention among themselves. Paul wrote that there was strife and division among them (1 Cor. 3:3). As he exposed this trap, he added that there were divisions and heresies among them (1 Cor. 11:18). The church had been instructed to walk in love (1 Cor. 13), but had failed to repent to one another. Thus, some were receiving the Lord's Supper in an unworthy manner. This strife was blocking God's healing power from manifesting among the believers in the church. The result was that many were weak and sickly, and many died because they did not discern the body of Christ!

As long as the early church taught the simple revelation of Christ's atoning work and walked in pure love and faith, there was a continual manifestation of healing that demonstrated the healing covenant. But when the flesh rose up, the result was weakness and sickness in the church. This is why Paul instructed the believers to judge (examine) themselves when receiving the Lord's Supper (1 Cor. 11:28). The Greek word for *examine* in this passage means to test yourself.[11] This inner searching turns the light on an individual's own flaws and weakness, causing that person to repent and confess his or her faults. This confessing of personal faults (sins; missing the mark) and praying for one another would lead to the blessing of healing.

> Confess your faults one to another, and pray one for another, that ye may be healed. The effectual fervent prayer of a righteous man availeth much.
>
> —JAMES 5:16

## NOT LIVING BY BREAD ALONE

The Scripture says, "It is written, That man shall not live by bread alone, but by every word of God" (Luke 4:4). We can receive the bread of Communion daily. However, we must also feed from the Scriptures and every word that comes from God. For example, if you receive the bread of Communion, yet in your heart you despise your brother, you are breaking the commandment of the new covenant to love and forgive your enemies (Matt. 5:44). If you have not forgiven those who have wronged you and you are claiming healing for yourself, you must first release the persons you are holding hostage in your heart and forgive them their trespasses (Matt. 6:12). We cannot expect the healing power of God to work in our lives if we are eating the bread alone and not walking in obedience to the Word of God.

This is why we are to confess our faults one to another, and pray for one another, that we may be healed (James 5:16). Christ is our example. Christ did not die on the cross until He first prayed, "Father, forgive them; for they know not what they do" (Luke 23:34). Christ knew that He could not die to redeem mankind from sin if He Himself died with unforgiveness toward those who had beaten and crucified Him. Even Stephen, while being stoned, asked God not to hold the sin of his death against those who murdered him (Acts 7:60). Both of these prayers had amazing results. At the moment Christ died, the cruel centurion became a believer, saying, "Truly this was the Son of God" (Matt. 27:54). A man assisting in the stoning of Stephen was Saul of Tarsus, who was later converted and became the great apostle Paul (Acts 7:58).

Obedience to the Word includes not only understanding and participating in Communion, but it also includes releasing anyone who has harmed us physically, emotionally, or spiritually. This is how we judge ourselves at the Lord's Table, by examining our relationship with both God and man.

We can clearly see that breaking of bread was a consistent, daily practice among the early Christians and was part of the Communion meal, which was administered from house to house. The bread represented the precious body of our Lord, which was beaten for our healing (Isa. 53:5; 1 Pet. 2:24). Scripture reveals that this process of Christ's atoning work did not begin on the cross but in the Garden of Gethsemane. Let us discover the secrets of redemption that began in the garden.

## FOR YOUR REFLECTION

1. List two references from the New Testament where they "broke bread."

   a. _____

   b. _____

2. Name three people who had churches in their homes

   a. Romans 16:5

   _____

   b. Colossians 4:15

   _____

   c. Philemon 2

   _____

3. Name five commentaries that teach breaking bread was daily communion.

   a. _____

   b. _____

   c. _____

   d. _____

   e. _____

4. Describe what a "love feast" was in the early church.

   _____

   _____

   _____

5.  What spiritual condition(s) hindered the "health" of the church at Corinth?

    a.  1 Corinthians 3:3

    _____

    b.  1 Corinthians 11:18

    _____

6.  What else must we do to obey God besides receiving the bread of Communion?

    _____

    _____

CHAPTER 4

# SECRETS IN THE GARDEN
# OF GETHSEMANE

And so it is written, The first man Adam was made a living soul; the last Adam was made a quickening spirit. *L AST ADAM* —1 CORINTHIANS 15:45

IN THE GARDEN OF Eden, the first Adam was not born through a normal birth process, and neither was the second Adam, Jesus Christ. The first Adam was formed from dust, and the second Adam was formed in the womb of a virgin (Gen. 2:7; Luke 1:27–31). The first Adam was perfect before the Fall, and the second Adam was sinless throughout this life (2 Cor. 5:21). The first Adam fell into sin while living in a garden, and the second Adam had the sins of the world placed upon him in a garden called Gethsemane. At the tree of the knowledge of good and evil the first Adam experienced death, and at a tree called a cross the second Adam experienced death. But through the cross, the second Adam conquered death, hell, and the grave and is alive forever more (Rev. 1:18). Eternal death began in a garden, and the plan of redemption began near the temple in Jerusalem, in a garden called Gethsemane.

There is a powerful mystery surrounding that fateful night of destiny in Gethsemane. This Jerusalem garden, nestled in a narrow valley between the Eastern Gate and the Mount of Olives, was a favorite retreat for Christ to come apart to reflect and pray (John 18:2). Some have suggested this garden may have been owned by a rich follower of Christ, perhaps Joseph of Arimathea, or Nicodemus, the rich man who visited Jesus secretly at night (John 3:1–15). Scripture indicates that Christ resorted there often with His disciples. On this night, the retreat would turn into an all-night intercession service.

It was in this very garden where Christ revealed to Nicodemus that, as Moses lifted the serpent in the wilderness, so He (Christ) would be lifted up (on the cross) to draw all men to Him (John 3:14). The story of the brass serpent in Numbers 21:2–9 is an amazing picture of the redemptive work of Christ. Israel had sinned and was bitten by serpents. As people lay dying, Moses constructed a brass serpent on a pole. All who looked to the brass snake lived! God chose a brass serpent to represent Christ, since brass represents humanity and the serpent represents sin. Christ became man and bore our sins on the tree!

Christ entered the garden and invited three of His disciples—Peter, James, and John—to participate in an important late-night prayer vigil. Weary from a busy week, the prayer support team fell asleep as Christ poured out His soul for one hour. Christ understood the coming events. His prayer turned into an agonizing three hours of intercession, until His sweat became as great drops of blood (Luke 22:44). This could happen only under extreme physical and mental stress as the blood capillaries expanded and allowed red blood to mingle with the salty sweat. The word *agony* comes from the root word *agon,* which alludes to a contest or a fight.[1]

What was actually occurring? I believe that during these three hours, the sins of mankind were being transferred upon Christ, just as in the Old Testament when Israel's sins were transferred to the scapegoat on the Day of Atonement. We see a reference to this transference of sins onto Christ in 2 Corinthians 5:21:

> For he hath made him to be sin for us, who knew no sin; that we might be made the righteousness of God in him.

> Him who knew no sin he made (to be) sin on our behalf; that we might become the righteousness of God in him.
> —2 CORINTHIANS 5:21, ASV

As the sins of the world weighed upon Christ, I believe He experienced an unbearable burden, causing Him to pray that if it were possible, that God would allow this cup of suffering to pass from Him (Matt. 26:42, 44). The two hours of agony were so intense that Paul wrote in Hebrews that this event almost killed Christ and He had to seek God to spare Him from premature death:

> Who in the days of his flesh, when he had offered up prayers and supplications with strong crying and tears unto him that was able to save him from death, and was heard in that he feared; Though he were a Son, yet learned he obedience by the things which he suffered.
>
> —HEBREWS 5:7–8

How did God save Him from death, since Christ died on the cross the following day? God spared Christ from dying in the garden, as the agonizing pressure was pressing the blood through His face. This event was foreseen by Isaiah when he wrote, "Thou shall make his soul an offering for sin....he shall bear their iniquities" (Isa. 53:10–11).

Isaiah further wrote about the suffering Messiah when he said:

> Surely he hath borne our griefs, and carried our sorrows: yet we did esteem him stricken, smitten of God, and afflicted.
>
> —ISAIAH 53:4

Over six hundred years later, Matthew recalled Isaiah's prophecy as being fulfilled through Jesus Christ as He was healing the sick:

> That it might be fulfilled which was spoken by Esaias the prophet, saying, Himself took our infirmities, and bare our sicknesses.
>
> —MATTHEW 8:17

In Isaiah 53, the English Bible speaks of "griefs" and "sorrows." Matthew correctly translates these Hebrew words as "infirmities" and "sicknesses." He reveals that Christ bore (carried in Him) our infirmities and sicknesses. Therefore, in the garden, He was made sin with our sins and sick with our sicknesses. Is it any wonder He was asking for this cup to pass? It was not just the cup of the cross, but it was also the sufferings He was experiencing in Gethsemane.

Christ knew, however, that His sufferings would accomplish a divine plan—to bring salvation and healing to those who would receive the new covenant. This atonement would impact the body, soul, and spirit of anyone who accepted the full atoning work of Christ.

## THE BODY, SOUL, AND SPIRIT

And the very God of peace sanctify you wholly; and I pray God your whole spirit and soul and body be preserved blameless unto the coming of our Lord Jesus Christ.

—1 THESSALONIANS 5:23

The physical body can become sick, the soul (mind) can experience negative emotions, and the human spirit can become tainted by sin through disobedience to God's Word. The atonement sets out to redeem the spirit, renew the soul, and restore or heal the body, causing a person to become whole or complete in Christ.

Isaiah breaks down how the sufferings of the Messiah will impact the tripartite nature of mankind:

### 1. The atonement of the body

Isaiah prophesied that, "With his stripes we are healed" (Isa. 53:5). Isaiah looks forward to the atoning work of the Messiah. Peter, however, looks back at the finished work of the cross and proclaims, "By whose stripes ye were healed" (1 Pet. 2:24).

### 2. The atonement of the soul

Isaiah revealed the atonement for the soul when he wrote, "He is despised and rejected of men; a man of sorrows, and acquainted with grief" (Isa. 53:3). Christ was also oppressed and afflicted (v. 7). Oppression, sorrow, and grief are all emotions that can wreck havoc on the emotions and minds of believers. Yet Christ carried sorrow and grief to the cross on our behalf.

### 3. The atonement of the spirit

The prophet then revealed that the Christ would be wounded for our transgressions and bruised for our iniquities (Isa. 53:5). In verse 10 he wrote, "Thou shalt make his soul an offering for sin." Sin is a spiritual disease that eats away at man's spirit. Christ's ultimate goal was to redeem the spirit of a person and impart the gift of eternal life.

Isaiah sums up the sufferings of the Messiah in the last two verses of Isaiah 53:

> He shall see of the travail of his soul, and shall be satisfied: by his knowledge shall my righteous servant justify many; for he shall bear their iniquities. Therefore will I divide him a portion with the great, and he shall divide the spoil with the strong; because he hath poured out his soul unto death: and he was numbered with the transgressors; and he bare the sin of many, and made intercession for the transgressors.
>
> —ISAIAH 53:11–12

Notice that He will bear their iniquities; Christ bore our sins. He poured out His soul unto death. He was numbered (hung) on a cross between two transgressors (thieves), and He made intercession for one thief who requested to be remembered when Jesus came into His kingdom (Luke 23:39–42). Jesus provided a complete redemptive work from the whipping post to the old rugged cross! The stripes on His back were for my physical healing, the thorns on His head provide for my mental and emotional well-being, and the suffering on the cross dealt a deathblow to sin and provided eternal life for my spirit.

## THREE MEN REPRESENT THE THREE LEVELS OF ATONEMENT

It is not by coincidence that Christ chose three men out of the twelve to be His inner circle that night in the garden. His three closest disciples—Peter, James, and John—each have a character trait that parallels the emotional, bodily, and spiritual atonement. Peter represented emotional atonement, James represented bodily atonement, and John represented spiritual atonement.

First, look at Peter. He continually needed a renewing of his emotions. Before Peter received the Holy Spirit, he was brash, arrogant, and self-centered. It was Peter who demanded to walk on the water with Jesus. Peter also rebuked Christ for predicting He would die in Jerusalem. He insisted that he would never deny Christ, but had little confidence the others would follow his strong stance for the Savior. To prove his loyalty, the quick and emotionally high-strung, sword-swinging follower of Jesus whacked the ear from the head of a high priest's servant. Hours later, however, his burning passion turned cold, when out of fear he denied the Lord three times. And to prove the point, he cursed a few lines (Matt. 26:69–75). Peter was an apostle, called of God, and yet he was emotionally unstable at times. Peter is a picture of a person who loves Christ but lives on an emotional roller coaster and needs stability.

One of the most detailed instructions in the New Testament that outlines how elders in the church should minister to the sick was penned by the apostle James:

> Is any sick among you? let him call for the elders of the church; and let them pray over him, anointing him with oil in the name of the Lord: And the prayer of faith shall save the sick, and the Lord shall raise him up; and if he have committed sins, they shall be forgiven him. Confess your faults one to another, and pray one for another, that ye may be healed. The effectual fervent prayer of a righteous man availeth much.
>
> —JAMES 5:14–16

This passage deals more with physical healing than spiritual healing. The prayers of the elders are designed for believers within the church. Sick individuals are to call for the elders. Please notice how confessing your faults one to another is linked to receiving your healing. James, the second of the inner circle disciples, gives the details of the physical or bodily atonement.

The third disciple was John. The Gospel of John gives the clearest and most detailed description of the suffering of Christ and His redeeming work through the cross. When new converts begin reading the Bible, ministers often suggest they begin with the Gospel of John. This friend of Christ was with Him in the garden.

He was a witness at the trial, and he stood at the foot of the cross with Mary when the others were hiding out of fear (John 18:16; 19:27). Thus John is the disciple whose theme is centered on the spiritual atonement of mankind.

The life and writings of these three disciples are significant because of the threefold impact that Christ's complete work would have on humanity: emotional healing, physical healing, and a complete spiritual redemption from sin.

## MYSTERIES IN THE GARDEN

Not only was sin and sickness being placed upon God's Lamb, Jesus Christ, but also Satan was interested in the activity taking place. Jesus made this clear when He was preparing for the conflict in the garden:

> Hereafter I will not talk much with you: for the prince of this world cometh, and hath nothing in me.
>
> —JOHN 14:30

The prince of the world was Satan himself. Apparently, Christ wanted His disciples to know that when His sweat became blood and when soldiers arrested Him, that it was not Satan's agenda but God's plan from the foundation of the world (Col. 1:26). This heavenly plan had been hid from ages past, but it was about to be known. God, however, hid the mystery from satanic powers:

> Which none of the princes of this world knew: for had they known it, they would not have crucified the Lord of glory.
>
> —1 CORINTHIANS 2:8

The passage indicates that Satan would have stopped Christ's death had he known the full impact it would have on his dark kingdom.

When Judas entered the garden with a band of six hundred Roman soldiers to seize Christ, the Savior was now prepared as the sin offering for the world (John 18:1–3). From this garden, situated just below the ancient temple altar, the Lamb of God was ready to be slain as the final sin offering. Sin seized Adam in the Garden of Eden, and sin was placed upon Christ in the Garden of

*HEALING* ↓

Gethsemane. It was not *His* sin but the sins of others that He would carry to the cross.

Jesus was a substitute for us, carrying both our diseases and our sins. While many churches emphasize only the forgiveness of sins, throughout the Bible and especially in the ministry of Jesus, He made no distinction between forgiveness and physical healing. In fact, healing and forgiveness went hand in hand. Christ told a man, "Thy sins are forgiven," and then He commanded the man to rise, take up his bed, and walk (Luke 5:20–25). James said that when a believer is healed, "if he have committed sins, they shall be forgiven him" (James 5:15).

The Passover Lamb in Exodus 12 and the brass serpent in Numbers 21 are just two of many types and shadows of Christ's atoning work. There is another picture of Christ as revealed in the manna that fell in the wilderness for forty years.

## FOR YOUR REFLECTION

1.  Who were the two Adams in Scripture?

     a. _____

     b. _____

2.  Describe what this chapter says was happening to Christ during His three hours of "agony" in the Garden of Gethsemane.

     _____

     _____

     _____

3.  Man is a tripartite being. Name the three parts of a human being:

     a. _____

     b. _____

     c. _____

4.  There were three men out of the twelve who were part of the inner circle of apostles praying with Jesus that night in the garden—Peter, James, and John. Each of these men represents one of the parts of a human being. Explain each apostle's representative part:

a.  Peter

_____

_____

b.  James

_____

_____

c.  John

_____

_____

CHAPTER 5

# THE MYSTERY OF THE MANNA

Then Jesus said unto them, Verily, verily, I say unto you, Moses gave you not that bread from heaven; but my Father giveth you the true bread from heaven.

—JOHN 6:32

IMAGINE ATTEMPTING TO FEED six hundred thousand men, along with women and children, living in tents in a desolate wilderness for forty years! There were no trains running from Egypt and no local bakeries. However, each morning, God provided supernatural bread called manna (Num. 11:9). This heavenly bread provided nourishment and sustained the Hebrews during their wilderness wanderings. This simple bread from heaven was a picture of the coming Messiah.

From the first day of the week (Sunday) to the sixth day of the week (Friday), small white droplets fell from heaven onto the ground and were collected early each morning. It fell like dew on the ground (Exod. 16:14). There is much spiritual symbolism surrounding this manna, which was called the bread from heaven and angel's food (Ps. 78:25). When Israel saw the small white wafers lying on the ground, they called it manna. The root word for manna in Hebrew is *mah*, which simply means "what."[1]

And when the children of Israel saw it, they said one to another, It is manna: for they wist not what it was.

—EXODUS 16:15

46

When the surprised Hebrews stepped out of their tents and saw the ground covered in white, they literally said, "What is it?" This was the first time God had sent His people bread from heaven. However, it would not be the last. Centuries later, Christ, the "true bread from heaven" would be sent to Earth, and multitudes would question, "Who is He? A man, a prophet, a god, or the Messiah?"

## THE CORIANDER SEED

The Bible gives a detailed description of the manna:

> And the house of Israel called the name thereof Manna: and it was like coriander seed, white; and the taste of it was like wafers made with honey.
>
> —EXODUS 16:31

> And the manna was as coriander seed, and the colour thereof as the colour of bdellium.
>
> —NUMBERS 11:7

The coriander seed is used today as a spice. During one of our telecasts with Dr. John Miller, he showed the viewer a bowl of coriander seeds that were painted white, which gave a perfect imagery of the manna God used to feed the people.

When you look closely at a coriander seed, you will observe small furors, or "stripes" on the outer shell.

When combining all of the information on the manna, we discover the following:

+ Manna was something Israel had never seen before.
+ Manna had the texture of a wafer.
+ Manna had a slight taste of honey.
+ Manna was similar to a coriander seed.
+ Manna fell during the night.
+ Manna was the color of bdellium—a pearly white.
+ Manna fell for six days.
+ A double portion fell on Friday.

In John chapter 6, Jesus spoke about the manna, or the bread God sent from heaven for Israel in the wilderness:

> Then Jesus said unto them, Verily, verily, I say unto you, Moses gave you not that bread from heaven; but my Father giveth you the true bread from heaven. For the bread of God is he which cometh down from heaven, and giveth life unto the world. Then said they unto him, Lord, evermore give us this bread. And Jesus said unto them, I am the bread of life: he that cometh to me shall never hunger; and he that believeth on me shall never thirst.
>
> —JOHN 6:32–35

Like the manna in the wilderness, Jesus was sent from the Father in heaven to Earth for God's people, Israel. Just as manna gave life to those on their journey, Christ came so that we might have life and have it more abundantly (John 10:10). Manna was something Israel had never seen before on Earth, and Christ was someone mankind had never seen before on earth. When Israel saw manna in the wilderness, they asked, "What is it?" When the people of Israel saw Christ, they wondered, "Who is He?"

Manna was white, a color that represents righteousness in the Bible (Rev. 19:8). The manna was striped, and Christ bore stripes on His body. Manna was to be eaten every day during Israel's journey, and Jesus is the true bread from heaven. If manna was eaten daily, then this is another pattern indicating how we can partake of the true bread from heaven each day through the bread and cup of the Communion meal.

It is interesting to note that God instructed Israel to gather a double portion of the manna on Friday so they would not need to work on the Sabbath day. On one occasion, the Hebrews attempted to store some for the next day, even though it wasn't the Sabbath, and the manna spoiled, began to stink, and produced worms. This is because the people disobeyed God and would not follow His instructions, just as today some believers begin to walk in disobedience and eventually bring the displeasure of God upon their lives.

## MANNA IN THE POT

Israel needed fresh manna daily, and any attempt to store it (except on Friday before the Sabbath) caused the manna to spoil. Moses, however, instructed the priest to place a golden pot with manna inside the ark of the covenant. Inside this gold box were three items: the manna, the rod of Aaron that had blossomed, and the two tablets of the law written on stone (Heb. 9:4). Each item represents a special blessing from God.

The manna represents salvation since Jesus is the bread of life and salvation brings eternal life. The tablets of law represent sanctification, a blessing that separates you from the power of sin controlling your life. Aaron's rod was used to produce miracles, which is a picture of the miracle-working power of the Holy Spirit.

The manna in the ark never spoiled during the entire journey of Israel in the wilderness. I believe this is because the tangible presence of God rested continually on the ark of the covenant; therefore, it was impossible for the manna to spoil as long as it remained in the ark of the covenant. Christ died and His body was wrapped in linen and laid in a tomb, but His body did not see corruption (Acts 2:27). According to historians, the body was placed on a large rectangular-shaped stone slab. At the resurrection, the disciples saw two angels sitting on the slab, one at the top and the other at the bottom where the body had laid. This imagery is a picture of the mercy seat on the ark of the covenant. It was a gold rectangular-shaped lid with two golden angels facing each other. The imagery in the tomb is the imagery of the mercy seat of the ark! Just as the manna did not corrupt in the ark in Moses's time, the body of Christ did not corrupt in the tomb!

## THE MANNA AND THE BODY OF CHRIST

During Christ's ministry, He broke bread with His disciples, and the early church broke bread from house to house. At the Last Supper, Christ took bread and said, "This is my body" (Mark 14:22). During the Communion supper, the bread is a picture of the body of Christ. The Bible says that He was wounded

for our transgressions and bruised for our iniquities (Isa. 53:5). These wounds
and bruises were physical marks placed upon Christ's body when He endured the
violent beating with a cat-o'-nine-tails, a short-handled whip with nine long, leather
straps embedded with pieces of metal. These wounds provide for our healing (v. 5).
Other wounds were caused by the piercing of nails in His hands and feet. The
cut in His side was created by the spear of the centurion. The preview to Christ's
beating can be seen in the wilderness manna.

## THE MANNA WAS BEATEN

Before the manna was eaten and the people received nourishment from the heavenly bread, it was necessary for the manna to be beaten and crushed:

> And the people went about, and gathered it, and ground it in mills, or beat
> it in a mortar, and baked it in pans, and made cakes of it: and the taste of it
> was as the taste of fresh oil.
> —NUMBERS 11:8

The wilderness manna was beaten, then baked in pans and eaten. Just as the wilderness bread from heaven was beaten, so was the eternal bread from heaven, Jesus
Christ. His flesh was cut into bloody ribbons to provide healing for mankind. The
beaten wilderness manna was then placed in a pan where a fire was used to bake
the manna. Christ predicted that after His death on the cross, He would descend
into the lower parts of the earth (Matt. 12:40; Eph. 4:8–10). Now, through the
Lord's Supper, we remember the Lord's body when we partake of the bread.

## THE HOAR FROST ON THE GROUND

Another beautiful picture of Christ's body and His atoning work is hidden in
the story of the wilderness manna. The Bible compares the manna to a hoar frost
coving the ground.

> And when the dew that lay was gone up, behold, upon the face of the wilder-
> ness there lay a small round thing, as small as the hoar frost on the ground.
> —EXODUS 16:14

Everyone is familiar with an early morning frost on the ground. But the phrase "hoar frost" is unique. The Hebrew root word for hoar frost is *kephowr*, a word that is akin to the word *kippur*.[2] Yom Kippur is the Hebrew phrase meaning the Day of Atonement, the sixth appointed season among Israel's seven feasts. It was the day when the high priest entered the holy of holies and sprinkled blood on the mercy seat of the ark of the covenant to atone for himself, the priests, and the people. The word atonement is mentioned eighty-one times in the Bible, and seventy-three of those times the Hebrew word is *kaphar*, meaning "to cover, to appease, and to purge."[3] The word describes the process that occurred after a sacrifice was offered before God. When the blood was poured out, God knew that it covered sin and purged the conscience of the offender. Many blood offerings were atonement offerings for sin and transgression. Since the hoar frost on the ground is a Hebrew word used to identify the Day of Atonement and means "to cover and appease," it was as though God was looking ahead in time when the true bread from heaven, Jesus Christ, would come down and spill His blood on the ground to atone for mankind!

Today, the Jewish bread used during Passover is a perfect picture of the body of Christ. This bread, called matzo bread, is white and shaped like a square, with long brown rows and holes piercing through the surface. This bread is baked without leaven (which represents sin) and is slightly browned on the surface. The lines running across the bread are a picture of the furrows placed in the back of Christ during the scourging. The holes represent the piercing the Messiah bore in His hands, feet, and side, while the brown spots remind us of the bruises on His body. The manna was like a coriander seed, which has small furrows over the surface. The manna was a picture of the beaten body of the coming Savior who would bring salvation and healing to those who would eat the true bread from heaven.

## THE TRUE BREAD

Just as the wilderness bread gave life and strength, sustaining the entire nation of Israel, the church, which is a chosen generation and a holy nation (1 Pet. 2:9), must continue in the life and strength of the Lord through His Word, His Spirit, and through a fresh understanding and revelation of the Communion meal. Christ made it clear in John chapter 6 that those who would partake of His blood and body would receive life and would be a part of the resurrection of the dead.

> Whoso eateth my flesh, and drinketh my blood, hath eternal life; and I will raise him up at the last day. For my flesh is meat indeed, and my blood is drink indeed. He that eateth my flesh, and drinketh my blood, dwelleth in me, and I in him.
>
> —JOHN 6:54–56

Imagine the response of the audience when Christ taught this in a Jewish synagogue. The Bible indicates that the multitude got up and walked out in the middle of the sermon! Jews do not eat blood in any form, according to the Law of Moses. Clearly, they misunderstood the message, as they did on other occasions. He was not speaking of literally eating His body and drinking His blood, just as when He spoke of destroying the temple and rebuilding it again He was not speaking of the temple in Jerusalem but about His own death and resurrection (John 2:19–21). Eating His flesh is the bread and drinking His blood is the fruit of the vine of the Communion supper.

## THE FRUIT OF THE VINE

When the New Testament speaks of wine, most people immediately picture a bottle of fermented wine. In the Bible, however, the word *wine* was also used to describe grapes when they are still hanging in a cluster (Isa. 65:8). In the Old Testament there are several different Hebrew words that distinguish between fermented and unfermented wine or strong drink. In the New Testament, however, there is one common word for wine, the Greek word *oinos*, which makes it difficult to distinguish between fermented and unfermented.

When Christ held up the cup at the Last Supper, He called it the "fruit of the vine" (Matt. 26:29; Mark 14:25; Luke 22:18). Grapes were called the fruit of the vine, and the pure grape was used at the supper. Jewish sources indicate that during a Jewish Passover Seder, three parts water is mixed with the wine so that any alcohol content is reduced significantly. They do this because children partake of the Passover Seder. The early church father Justin Martyr, when giving instructions for Holy Communion, wrote, "Thereafter the supervisor receives the cup, in which the wine and water are mixed," indicating that the Passover cup used Communion in his day was a mixture of wine and water, as was used in a Jewish Seder, according to the *Commentary on the New Testament From the Talmud and Hebraica*.[4]

The mixing of wine with water is unique when you consider that at the crucifixion, Christ shed all of His blood, and when the centurion thrust the spear into Christ's side, both blood and water came forth (John 19:34). At the ancient tabernacle and Jewish temples, two substances were the water in the laver and the blood on the altar. Jesus was baptized in water, His sweat (water) was mixed with His blood at Gethsemane, and on the cross the blood and water poured down His side. Consider the parallel of how our redemptive process comes through faith in Christ's blood and how it is sealed in the water of baptism!

> This is he that came by water and blood, even Jesus Christ; not by water only, but by water and blood. And it is the Spirit that beareth witness, because the Spirit is truth. For there are three that bear record in heaven, the Father, the Word, and the Holy Ghost: and these three are one. And there are three that bear witness in earth, the spirit, and the water, and the blood: and these three agree in one.
>
> —1 JOHN 5:6–8

The bread eaten at both Passover and Communion has no leaven, because leaven represents sin (1 Cor. 5:7–8). Christ was a sinless sacrifice:

> But with the precious blood of Christ, as of a lamb without blemish and without spot.
>
> —1 PETER 1:19

Being born of a virgin, Christ's blood was not tainted with the original sin of Adam, since the seed of a human man was not needed to conceive the Son of God.

Because of His sinless blood (1 Pet. 1:19), I personally believe that it is best to use the pure blood of the grape, or grape juice, when receiving Communion. In order for grape juice to ferment and create alcohol, it needs a breakdown of the sugar to create bacteria. And bacteria in the juice would be like leaven in the bread. To me, this would imply that Christ's pure and sinless blood was corrupted in some form, thus limiting the power of His redemptive blood as a sinless offering.

In John 15:1, Christ declared He was the true vine, and in John 6:32–35, He said He was the true bread from heaven. The fruit of the vine in the cup could only be received when the grapes were crushed to form the juice or the wine. Earthly bread is made from the grain of crushed wheat. Jesus compared His death to a grain of wheat falling into the ground and dying, else it abides alone; but if it dies, it will bring forth much fruit (John 12:24). Both the wheat and the grapes had to be crushed for the bread and the fruit of the vine, just as Christ had to be wounded, bruised, and crucified to bring forth a covenant of eternal life.

## THE TABLE OF SHOWBREAD

In the tabernacle in the wilderness and in both Jewish temples, the priests prepared holy bread that was placed on a gold table called the table of showbread. The table was positioned in the second sacred chamber called the holy place, against the northern wall. There were twelve individual pieces of bread representing the twelve tribes of Israel (Lev. 24:5). Each week the priests prepared the flour by crushing the wheat and sifting the fine flour twelve times.[5] The bread was baked with oil and frankincense. Each week the bread was eaten by the priests, and fresh bread was baked for the table each week. Numbers 4:7 says that bread should be upon the table continually.

The Hebrew word for showbread means the "bread of face,"[6] because the table of bread was located close to the veil—the curtain that separated the holy place from the holy of holies. The bread was eaten weekly throughout the year. This imagery reminds the believer of the importance of each week, during the Sabbath, receiving the bread of the Word in your local church. Fresh bread was baked every week, and believers need fresh manna each week.

We again see the importance of both the holy bread and of receiving the bread. In summary:

+ The manna was bread made in heaven; Christ came from heaven.
+ The manna sustained the Hebrew nation; Christ sustains those in covenant with Him.
+ The manna was to be eaten daily; we can receive Communion daily.
+ The showbread was prepared weekly and eaten on the Sabbath; we need weekly bread.

Now that we understand the significance of the bread from heaven and the importance of daily Communion, we must explore why an individual believer has the spiritual authority to partake of the sacrament, even if they are not a priest or an ordained minister. The secret is found in the priesthood of the believer.

### FOR YOUR REFLECTION

1. There are several characteristics of the manna in the wilderness that are symbolic of Jesus Christ. Below each characteristic of manna listed below, explain how it symbolically points us to Jesus Christ.

   a. Manna was pure white.

   _____

   _____

   b. The coriander seed from which manna was made has stripes.

   _____

   _____

   c. Manna was to be eaten every day.

   _____

   _____

    d.  A portion of manna was to be kept inside the ark of the covenant in the most holy place in the tabernacle.

_____

_____

2.  Another symbolism found in the story of the manna in the wilderness is found in the Hebrew word for "hoar frost," in Exodus 16:14, which is *kephowr*. How does the meaning of this word point us to Jesus Christ?

_____

_____

_____

3.  Jewish matzo bread, used today in the celebration of Passover, also has characteristics that symbolically point us to Jesus. Describe the symbolism of the matzo bread on the lines below.

_____

_____

_____

# CHAPTER 6

# THE PRIESTHOOD OF THE BELIEVER

But ye are a chosen generation, a royal priesthood, an holy nation, a peculiar people; that ye should shew forth the praises of him who hath called you out of darkness into his marvellous light.

—1 PETER 2:9

IN ANCIENT ISRAEL GOD established an earthly priesthood to receive tithe, offer sacrifices, oversee the tabernacle and later both Jewish temples in Jerusalem, and stand as a bridge linking heaven and Earth, God and man. The mysterious Melchizedek was the first king-priest of God in Abraham's day. Four hundred years later, Moses's brother, Aaron, initiated the Aaronic priesthood in the time of the tabernacle. Centuries later in the days of Solomon, a faithful priest named Zadok formed the Zadok priesthood (Ezek. 48:11). The Jewish priesthood came to an abrupt end at the destruction of the temple in A.D. 70.

## THE BAPTISM OF JESUS

However, the true priesthood was transferred long before A.D. 70, and the process began when Jesus, at age thirty, stepped into the Jordan River to be baptized.

John the Baptist, the cousin of Christ, was the son of a priest named Zacharias who served in the temple in Jerusalem (Luke 1:9–13). John was baptizing believers at the Jordan River in an area called Bethabara (John 1:28). This was the same location where, fifteen hundred years earlier, Joshua had crossed the Jordan River and instructed the Hebrews to take twelve smooth stones out of the Jordan River and build a monument on the Israel side of the river as a memorial and reminder that God opened the Jordan River for them to cross. The priest also lifted twelve stones from the wilderness and placed these in the dried riverbed (Josh. 4:1–10). That day the water from the Jordan River was rolled back all the way to a city called Adam, ten miles away and south toward the Dead Sea (Josh. 3:16).

The area where Joshua crossed is the same area where John baptized Jesus, and it has powerful prophetic significance. When a high priest was preparing to transfer the priesthood to his son, there was a threefold procedure:

1.  The high priest's son had to submerge in water for purification (Lev. 8:6).
2.  The holy oil was to be poured upon the head of the high priest's son (Lev. 8:12).
3.  The high priest had to publicly declare that this was his son (Num. 20:28).

This three-part process occurred when Christ waded into the Jordan River. Christ stepped into the same area where Joshua had crossed. Joshua's Hebrew name was Yeshuah, and Jesus's actual Hebrew name is Yeshuah. In Joshua's time, the waters of the Jordan were rolled back to the city of Adam, just as Christ's redemptive work removed mankind's sins all the way back to the first man, Adam. When Christ stepped into the cold waters of the Jordan, He was being recognized by John, who was the son of a Jewish priest. Christ was not being baptized for the remission of sins because He was sinless. There is a deeper meaning to this baptism. Christ was thirty years of age—the same age that a Levite entered the priesthood (Num. 4:30). Little did Israel know that the priesthood in Jerusalem was being transferred to one man—Jesus Christ! That pattern is seen in His baptism.

1.  Christ was baptized in water, symbolic of preparation for the priesthood.

2.  The Spirit descended upon Him like a dove; this was the anointing (Matt. 3:16).
3.  God spoke from heaven, declaring that Jesus was His son (Matt. 3:17).

### SUPERNATURAL SIGNS APPEAR

From that moment, at age thirty, Christ preached repentance and demonstrated the kingdom of God, forgiving the sinner and healing the sick and diseased. From that moment, Jewish history records numerous signs at the temple, which demonstrate that the favor of the Lord was no longer upon the rituals. There are certain things that the Jewish Talmud says began to occur in A.D. 30, about the same time that Christ began His public ministry.

According to the Jewish Talmud (Yoma 39), supernatural signs began happening in the temple when Simeon the Righteous served as high priest during a forty-year period. After his death, they continued from time to time and were a good sign to the Jews. These good signs manifested about 300 B.C., in the time of Alexander the Great.

However, around A.D. 30, about forty years prior to the destruction of the temple, the following strange signs began to occur.

The first sign involved the Day of Atonement. On that day the high priest stood before two identical goats. He drew lots, which were a *black and a white pebble* from a golden urn (Yoma 4:1, 37). The black stone was marked for Azazel, and the white stone was marked for the Lord. When the lot marked for the Lord came up in the right hand of the priest, it was a good omen. But from about A.D. 30 onward, it never came up in the right hand of the priest again.

On the Day of Atonement, *three scarlet straps* were used: one was tied to horns of the scapegoat and the second strap was tied around the neck of the goat for the Lord. The third red strap was nailed to the temple door. In the days of Simeon, the red thread supernaturally turned white, fulfilling Isaiah 1:18: "Though your sins be as scarlet, they shall be white as snow; though they be red like crimson, they shall be as wool." From A.D. 30 forward, the crimson strap never turned white again.

In the holy place sat *the golden seven-branched candelabra* called the menorah. Each morning the seven wicks were cleaned and fresh oil was added. The western branch was the closest to the holy of holies and was the first branch lit after the cleaning process. The other six candles were lit from the western light. In Simeon's day the western candle burned continually, even when the others went out. In A.D. 30, the western candle began to go out first.

At the temple was a large square, brass altar where the animal sacrifices were burnt. According to Jewish sources, only *two logs* supernaturally burnt on the altar, and no more wood was added throughout the day. After the year A.D. 30, more logs were needed to maintain the fire.

Another odd incident is reported concerning *the bread the priest ate* from the table of showbread. In the days of Simeon the Righteous, the priests were all given a piece of bread the size of a pea and were satisfied. After A.D. 30, the priest received a piece the size of a bean since the smaller portion no longer satisfied.

While Jewish rabbis questioned the meaning of these strange signs occurring forty years before the destruction of the temple, I believe that when we understand that the priesthood was being transferred at the Jordan River, near the same time frame, then we can understand the true significance of these signs.

## THE MEANING OF THE SIGNS

On the Day of Atonement, when the stone for the Lord came up in the wrong hand, it was an indicator that the sins being transferred on the scapegoat would no longer be acceptable, since the Lamb of God was now on the scene (John 1:29). The red thread no longer turning white was a message that no scapegoat would again bear our sins and carry them away; only Christ would bare our sins (1 Pet. 2:24). The candle near the holy of holies going out demonstrated that a new light of the world was in the earth (John 8:12). The fire on the altar would be replaced by the Holy Spirit's fire (Matt. 3:11). The bread from the table would no longer satisfy since the bread from heaven was now among men! These temple signs indicated a change.

## CHRIST THE NEW HIGH PRIEST

Another powerful incident also reveals how the Jewish priesthood was moving from the traditional priest to the new heavenly priestly order being established by God through Jesus Christ. In the time of Christ, Caiaphas was the high priest (Matt. 26:3). We are often taught that the priests wanted Christ dead because the leaders hated him and felt he was a threat. Yet, the words of Caiaphas reveal a different view. After the raising of Lazarus from the dead, Jewish leaders—men with the Pharisees and chief priest—were concerned that Jesus could cause an uprising that would lead to the Roman Empire taking over Jerusalem and removing the spiritual leaders from power. At that moment the high priest spoke a prophetic word:

> And one of them, named Caiaphas, being the high priest that same year, said unto them, Ye know nothing at all, nor consider that it is expedient for us, that one man should die for the people, and that the whole nation perish not. And this spake he not of himself: but being high priest that year, he prophesied that Jesus should die for that nation; and not for that nation only, but that also he should gather together in one the children of God that were scattered abroad. Then from that day forth they took counsel together for to put him to death.
>
> —JOHN 11:49–53

Caiaphas knew the Old Testament prophecies, including Isaiah's prediction of the suffering Messiah (Isa. 53:1–12). John said Caiaphas prophesied that Jesus should die for the nation. From that moment, they took counsel to put Him to death! Later, after His arrest, Jesus stood before Caiaphas, who demanded to know if Jesus was the Son of God (Matt. 26:63). Jesus answered, "You have said..." It appears Jesus knew that Caiaphas at some time had said (perhaps privately) that Jesus was the Son of God. Jesus then said, "Hereafter shall ye see the Son of man sitting on the right hand of power, and coming in the clouds of heaven" (v. 64).

Caiaphas immediately ripped his garment and said Christ had blasphemed. Ripping the garment demonstrated his anger, but from a Jewish perspective there was a more powerful symbolism in this action. The high priest garments were made with a special woven opening in the neck to prevent the garment from ever being ripped:

> You shall make the robe of the ephod all of blue. There shall be an opening for his head in the middle of it; it shall have a woven binding all around its opening, like the opening in a coat of mail, so that it does not tear.
>
> —EXODUS 28:31–32, NKJV

If a priest was to be expelled from his priestly office, the high priest would rip the front collar of the garment as a public witness that the man's priestly ministry was no longer valid. When Caiaphas ripped his own priestly garment, he, by the tradition of the Jews, voided his own office as high priest. As high priest, he was scheduled to oversee the offerings of the lambs at the upcoming Passover. We can assume that Caiaphas knew the reason for Christ's coming and that, in order to forgive sins, Christ was God's Son and would suffer death. Thus, another example is given of the transfer of the priesthood—by the high priest himself.

The following day, at three o'clock in the afternoon, Christ hung between heaven and Earth. Breathing His last breath He cried out, "It is finished." These three words were the same words used by a high priest at Passover when the final lamb was offered! Christ was the final offering. At that moment, the earth quaked and the huge veil in the temple hiding the holy of holies from man's view was ripped from top to bottom. That moment God opened His door for a new priestly order after the order of Melchizedek (Heb. 6:20), the first priest who had met Abraham near the place where Christ was being crucified!

No Jewish priest was ever a king and a priest. These were two separate offices held by two separate individuals. Only Melchizedek was the king of Jerusalem and a priest of the Most High God. This is why God chose Christ as a new order of the Melchizedek priesthood. Christ has been the High Priest in heaven for almost two thousand years, and, during His one-thousand-year reign on earth, He will be the King of kings (Rev. 19:16).

## THE HEAVENLY TEMPLE

If Christ is the High Priest and there is no longer a physical temple in the holy city of Jerusalem, then at what temple is Christ directing His priestly ministry? Paul wrote that Christ entered the temple in heaven by His own blood and now sits on the right hand of God, ever living to make intercession on our behalf (Heb. 7:21–25). On the yearly Day of Atonement, the high priest would minister from morning to evening, continually standing on his feet. Only when God declared that Israel's sins were remitted could the high priest, late that evening, sit down and rest.

When Stephen was being stoned to death, he saw a vision and said, "I see the heavens opened, and the Son of man standing on the right hand of God" (Acts 7:56). Yet Paul declared that Christ is seated on the right hand of the throne (Heb. 12:2). One man saw Christ *standing*, and another said He is *sitting*. I believe the reason Stephen saw Christ standing is because when the ancient high priest made intercession for sins, he stood before the presence of God. Stephen was praying a prayer, asking the Lord to forgive those who were stoning him:

> And he kneeled down, and cried with a loud voice, Lord, lay not this sin to their charge. And when he had said this, he fell asleep.
>
> —ACTS 7:60

Jesus was standing as the High Priest in the temple in heaven, making intercession because Stephen did not want those killing him to be charged for his death. Stephen forgave his enemies. Christ the High Priest stood up in the heavenly temple to forgive Stephen's enemies, and I believe to receive Stephen's spirit. This prayer asking forgiveness was so powerful that one man directing Stephen's execution, Saul of Tarsus, would later convert to Christ and become the apostle Paul (Acts 7:58; 13:9). It was Paul who taught that Christ was seated, indicating that the atoning work was complete.

## THE PRIESTHOOD OF THE BELIEVER

This brings us to the priesthood of the believer, a concept that has only been understood in contemporary times. The traditional Christian church has placed all spiritual responsibilities for church ministry solely upon the fivefold ministry (Eph. 4:11), especially the local pastor. My father pastored three different congregations when I was between the ages of three and eighteen. The people were wonderful believers. However, most had a mentality of expecting the pastor to fill the role of preacher, teacher, evangelist, janitor, choir director, counselor, intercessor, greeter, and parking attendant. Often the attitude seemed to be, "Let the preacher do it all, because isn't that what we pay him to do?" This narrow thinking was a lack of understanding the full plan of ministry that God has for His people.

In the first century, individuals had churches in their homes, and deacons were appointed to perform business tasks so the ministers could concentrate on praying and studying (Acts 6:3–4). In reality, every believer was a witness for Christ, and every believer could participate in some form of ministry. Some believers provided shelter for traveling ministers, some provided food, and others, such as Dorcas, made clothing for widows in her city (Acts 9:36–39). Paul referred to the faithful believers who loved the ministry and worked for God's kingdom as "saints." From Acts 9:13 to Revelation 20:9, the word *saint* is mentioned sixty times. All sixty references use the same Greek word, *hagios,* which means morally pure, consecrated, and blameless.[1]

## REMOVING THE BELIEVERS' PRIESTHOOD

After the first several centuries in the Christian church, certain traditions of the church fathers and opinions of church bishops and spiritual leaders began to reduce the involvement of common people in the local church. Eventually, men and women attended weekly service, gave their financial support, confessed their sins, prayed, and followed a liturgical routine. Most church ministerial activities remained under the control of trained ministers, who eventually felt that anyone without the proper theological or seminary training and ministerial experience had no right or authority to participate in ministry. This belief would have also influenced the tradition of house-to-house Communion. Eventually, in the year 325, the counsel of Nicea stated the following concerning Passover: "It appeared an unworthy thing that in this celebration of this most holy feast we should follow the practice of the Jews."[2] From that moment, the Hebraic-Jewish roots of the Christian faith began to be ripped from the ground and a more Greek-Roman system replaced the original foundation of our faith.

Eventually, the word *saint* became an exclusive term reserved for a select group of individuals. The Roman Church developed a list of qualifications to identify a true saint. However, in the New Testament, a saint was a holy person who had consecrated his or her life to God and was actively involved in praying, giving, teaching, and walking in the truth of God's Word. In several of Paul's letters to other believers, he mentioned, "The saints greet you" (Rom. 16:15; 2 Cor. 13:13; Phil. 4:22; Heb. 13:24). True believers who were faithful to Christ and walked in the new covenant were considered saints in the first-century church.

## WHO ARE THE PRIESTS?

If the first issue was, who are the saints? then the second issue is, who are the priests? There are several world religions that use priests and have developed a form of priesthood. The Buddhist religion has priests, or men who have committed themselves entirely to live at their temples and concentrate on prayers and study of their religion. In the Roman Catholic Church, there is an order of priests, bishops, and cardinals. Following a set order, a man can move from one level to a higher level. In the traditional Protestant churches, most leaders recognize three of the fivefold ministries in the church: pastor, teacher, and evangelist.

Certainly, God calls individuals into the ministry and has appointed individuals in the body of Christ as ministers of God, preaching, teaching, and instructing. However, look at a passage from the Book of Revelation:

> And from Jesus Christ, who is the faithful witness, and the first begotten
> of the dead, and the prince of the kings of the earth. Unto him that loved

us, and washed us from our sins in his own blood, and hath made us kings
and priests unto God and his Father; to him be glory and dominion for ever
and ever. Amen.
—REVELATION 1:5–6

Looking at other translations of verse 6, notice the emphasis:

And formed us into a kingdom (a royal race), priests to His God and Father—
to Him be the glory and the power and the majesty and the dominion
throughout the ages and forever and ever. Amen (so be it).
—AMP

And has made us to be a kingdom and priests to serve his God and Father—to him be glory and power for ever and ever! Amen.
—NIV

In John's apocalyptic vision, he described Christ as wearing a white garment
with a golden sash and standing in the midst of a golden menorah (Rev. 1:12–16).
This is a description of a high priest who exchanged his eight garments of glory
to those of white linen garments when he entered the holy of holies on the Day of
Atonement! John was seeing Christ as the heavenly High Priest standing in the
heavenly temple!

This is when John reveals (as the Greek text renders it), "He has made us a
kingdom of priests!" Not just, "kings and priests," but a kingdom of priests.
Forming a kingdom of priests was God's original plan for Israel when they came
out of Egypt. The Almighty said:

And ye shall be unto me a kingdom of priests, and an holy nation. These are
the words which thou shalt speak unto the children of Israel.
—EXODUS 19:6

God intended for every Hebrew to be a worshiper and enjoy His presence.
However, they failed by worshiping the golden calf and later fell into the same sins
of the pagan nations that remained in the Promised Land. During Israel's failures,
the Levites continued their religious rituals, but because of Israel's national sins,

God at times said He did not receive their offerings and sacrifices. (See the Books of Haggai and Malachi.)

After Christ ascended to heaven as the new heavenly priest and sealed the promises of the new covenant with His blood, He also initiated an earthly priesthood, or a new kingdom of priests! Every believer is an individual priest, and the church is the kingdom of priests that is overseen by the High Priest, Jesus Christ, from the heavenly temple! This is what Peter meant when he wrote:

> But ye are a chosen generation, a royal priesthood, an holy nation, a peculiar people; that ye should shew forth the praises of him who hath called you out of darkness into his marvellous light.
>
> —1 Peter 2:9

Melchizedek was the only king and priest in Old Testament history. Jesus followed the pattern and became a king and priest after the order of Melchizedek. Scripture says that we are a royal priesthood. Kings and priests minister, but kings rule. Today we offer sacrifices of praise and financial gifts, but in the future, we will rule and reign with Him for one thousand years. We are called a kingdom of priests and a holy nation. The church has carried on God's original plan for ancient Israel. Every believer is a minister unto the Lord.

There are some who teach that Communion should never be served by a layperson or a common Christian—but *only* by an ordained minister, a priest, or someone who has been trained to serve in ministry. However, if we are now priests unto God, then we have been given the spiritual authority of the priesthood through the new covenant to receive the bread and body of Christ. It is the traditions of men and the church that restrain the members of the church from becoming priests unto God.

## The Power of the Personal Priesthood

As a personal priest we can boldly approach the heavenly temple with our petitions. If we sin, we no longer go to a mortal man and confess our sins. The Bible says, "If any man sin, we have an advocate with the Father," and "If we confess our sins, he is faithful and just to forgive us our sins, and to cleanse us from all unrigh-teousness" (1 John 2:1; 1:9). Under the old order, a priest would burn incense, rep-resenting our prayers reaching up to God (Ps. 141:2). In the new order priesthood, every believer can offer prayers of supplication and thanksgiving and personal requests to God (Phil. 4:6). Under the old covenant the Levites received the tithe and presented it to God, but the Bible says that now, when we now give our offer-ing, Christ receives our gifts in heaven (Heb. 7:8).

My great-grandfather, Pete Bava, was a Catholic who came to America from Italy. He spoke with a strong Italian accent and wore a black suit, white shirt, black tie, and a black hat to church. In his younger days in Italy, he was familiar with the local priests and the operation of the church. Years later, after immigrating to America, he was stricken with a deadly disease that paralyzed him. The doctors gave him up to die. His two sons, John and Joe, had encountered two full-gospel ministers who were holding revivals in the community. The ministers believed and taught a message of healing through faith in Christ. Pete's two sons invited the preachers over to speak to their dad about healing. Pete was suspicious and skepti-cal, but in his dying condition he had nothing to lose. On minister asked him, "If we pray for you, Mr. Bava, and God heals you, will you serve Him?" In broken English, Pete replied, "If you can pray and God heals me, I'll serve God."

His son John, who later became my grandfather, told me that as the two min-isters prayed, Pete's bed began to shake, and the power of the Lord fell upon him. Suddenly Pete jumped out of the bed and began to shout, "I'm healed, I'm healed!" Pete lived another sixty years and died at age ninety-five in a nursing home, still smiling when he heard someone speak the name of Jesus.

## THE IMPORTANCE OF SPIRITUAL LEADERSHIP

Just as God established a divine order of a high priest, Levites (priests), and Israelites, likewise Christ has established an order of spiritual authority in the body of Christ. Most Protestant denominations offer an ordination to their licensed ministers if, over a period of time, they follow certain denominational stipulations, educational requirements, and biblical guidelines. For example, I am an ordained bishop in a major denomination. The denomination gives a bishop the opportunity to be elected by other bishops to high-level boards and positions within the denomination. Part of the duties of a bishop includes baptizing converts, uniting couples in holy matrimony, and giving the Sacrament (Communion) to believers in the church. In a local church setting, the pastor or an ordained bishop should certainly direct the order of the service and the giving of the Communion Supper. Paul wrote to Timothy about the requirements of a bishop:

> This is a true saying, If a man desire the office of a bishop, he desireth a good work. A bishop then must be blameless, the husband of one wife, vigilant, sober, of good behaviour, given to hospitality, apt to teach; not given to wine, no striker, not greedy of filthy lucre; but patient, not a brawler, not covetous; one that ruleth well his own house, having his children in subjection with all gravity; (for if a man know not how to rule his own house, how shall he take care of the church of God?) not a novice, lest being lifted up with pride he fall into the condemnation of the devil. Moreover he must have a good report of them which are without; lest he fall into reproach and the snare of the devil.
>
> —1 TIMOTHY 3:1–7

In Paul's instructions, he listed the moral character for a candidate of bishop, but he never listed the specific ministerial responsibilities of a bishop. We all know an ordained minister can baptize believers in water. However, Paul wrote to the church at Corinth that God did not send him to baptize but to preach the gospel (1 Cor. 1:17). There is no biblical reference to Paul ever conducting a wedding in the early church. We do know, however, that he spoke about the Lord's Supper to the church at Corinth (1 Cor. 11:20–30). My point is, even though a bishop is honored to give the Sacrament, the apostle Paul does not list the giving of the Lord's Supper as one of the duties of a bishop. I believe this is because the priesthood of the believer was understood by the Jewish believers within the local church and the believers traveled from house to house partaking in the Communion meal.

## YOUR BODY IS THE TEMPLE

Christ forewarned that the destruction of the temple was coming. Years prior to the destruction of the Jewish temple by the Roman Tenth Legion, Paul wrote the following words:

> Know ye not ye are the temple of God, and that the Spirit of God dwelleth in you?
>
> —1 CORINTHIANS 3:16

From the time of Moses, God's glory had been linked to the tabernacle of Moses and the first and second temples in Jerusalem. The temple was the meeting place for the five main offerings mentioned in the Torah, for the feasts to be celebrated, and for the new moon and Sabbath offerings. Christ knew that at the moment of His resurrection, the daily routines and rituals at the temple that had been practiced for fifteen hundred years from the time of Moses were now a reflection and a type and shadow of what had come—Jesus, the mediator of the new covenant. In a few years the large ashlars surrounding Jerusalem would be penetrated by Roman battering rams. The wooden gates would be opened to Roman armies, and the beautiful white temple would be charred black with the smell of burning wood. The temple would be no more.

Yet the temple still existed—in another form. It was a moving temple, like a portable tent that could go from city to city, town to town, and community to community. The physical body of the individual believer was now the temple of the Holy Spirit. The temple had three areas, and the human body is a tripartite being.

| THE TEMPLE IN JERUSALEM | THE HUMAN BODY |
|---|---|
| The outer court | The body (1 Thess. 5:23) |
| The inner court | The soul (1 Thess. 5:23) |
| The holy of holies | The spirit (1 Thess. 5:23) |

## Repairing the House of God

Both the tabernacle and the temples occasionally needed repairs. The weather in Jerusalem fluctuates throughout the year, and adverse weather conditions wreak havoc on wood, causing it to expand and contract, then eventually crack. For this reason the temple wood occasionally needed to be replaced or cracks needed repair. Part of the priestly activity was keeping the temple updated and in top condition. For example:

+ Priests were appointed to examine the wood that was used on the altar.
+ Each morning a priest cleaned the ashes off the altar from the previous day's sacrifices.
+ After a major feast, the priest washed the temple floor with water to remove the blood.
+ The altar had to be whitewashed before feasts to cover the blood of previous sacrifices.
+ The priest had to continually wash before presenting certain offerings before the Lord.
+ The animal blood was caught in silver vessels and carried to the altar to be poured out.
+ The fires had to continually burn on the altar and were to never go out.

It was not only the physical structure that needed attention, but the interior of the house was also under constant watch for any needed repairs. Whenever a wall needed repair in the holy of holies, the priest was placed in a box with one opening that faced the wall of the holy place. He was lowered by rope to fix the troubled spot. He was not permitted to look around the sacred chamber for fear of death.[3]

The massive veil hanging between the inner sanctum and the holy of holies was made to be a handbreadth thick and consisted of seventy-two squares sewn together. It is written that a team of oxen once attempted unsuccessfully to pull the veil apart. This veil was stitched together by young virgins who had a special room in the temple just for this activity.[4] Each year on Yom Kippur (the Day of Atonement), the high priest sprinkled blood on this veil. Every two years this veil had to be replaced because it eventually began to sag in the middle.

One of Israel's kings understood the principle of keeping God's house in proper working order. His name was Hezekiah, and his story is interesting. The king was a godly leader who was loved by his people. He was suddenly afflicted with a sore (perhaps cancer) that caused him to be sick unto death, according to 2 Kings 20:1. The prophet Isaiah instructed the king to set his house in order, for he would die and not live. When the prophet departed, Hezekiah turned his face to the wall and began crying out to God for mercy and extension of his life (v. 3). Before Isaiah departed from the courtyard, God heard King Hezekiah's prayer and sent the prophet back into the palace to announce, "I have heard your prayers and have seen your tears; I will add fifteen more years to your days." (See 2 Kings 20:5–6.)

Hezekiah could have passed away, but he received a new lease on life through prayer. Notice, however, that the prophet instructed the king to take a lump of figs and place them on the boil (v. 7). The mixture of prayer and a good home remedy brought healing to the king.

## REPAIRING THE TEMPLE

The Lord told Isaiah the king would die, yet God changed His mind. Why? I believe it was Hezekiah's concern for the temple of God that brought God's favor to him in time of crisis. Hezekiah was twenty-five years old when he began his reign in Jerusalem. During his first year, the king observed that the priests had allowed the temple to deteriorate. The doors of the temple porch were closed, the menorah was not lit, and the priests were not burning incense. Hezekiah immediately began to reestablish the correct procedure for caring for the house of God:

> He in the first year of his reign, in the first month, opened the doors of the house of the LORD, and repaired them.
>
> —2 CHRONICLES 29:3

Hezekiah commanded the priests to carry forth the filthiness out of the holy place (v. 5). We are told the priests went into the inner part of God's house to remove the junk that had accumulated.

> And the priests went into the inner part of the house of the LORD, to cleanse it ,and brought out all the uncleanness that they found in the temple of the LORD into the court of the house of the LORD. And the Levites took it, to carry it out abroad into the brook Kidron.
>                                                    —2 CHRONICLES 29:16

The junk in the temple was then dumped into the Kidron Brook. This small stream of water began near the Temple Mount and wove its wave through the rugged Judean Hills, eventually emptying into the Dead Sea. Later, when King Hezekiah was sick unto death, he turned his face to the wall and prayed. Literally, he turned toward the direction of the temple and prayed facing the holy of holies. This was the direction Solomon taught the Jews to pray when they were in trouble. I believe because Hezekiah demonstrated his concern for God's temple, then God demonstrated His concern for Hezekiah's physical temple.

## REPAIRING YOUR TEMPLE

People allow certain things to enter their body that are known to cause sickness and disease. Smoking still causes various forms of cancer. Alcohol still destroys brain cells. Illegal drugs slowly deteriorate brain cells and organs of the body. Age alone requires that we spend more time caring for our physical temple.

Sometimes it may not be what we are eating but what is eating us that weakens our bodies. Medical researchers say that, when a person becomes angry, the anger has a negative effect on the human body and can actually shut down the immune system for about six hours. A person who is continually angry can shut down the natural defense system in their body for hours or for days. Hospitals are filled with men and women who have used their mouths to devour other men and women who have offended them. Now a sickness has crept into their body, and they are attempting to cure a problem with medicine that may be removed only by the surgery of forgiveness, prayer, and confession.

Remember that confession of our faults and sins is required before receiving the blessed Lord's Supper. Also, the meal that heals should not simply become a ritual and another religious formula, and certainly it should never be viewed as some type of magical formula for healing.

## FOR YOUR REFLECTION

1. This chapter describes the symbolism behind the Jewish traditions and requirements for transferring the priesthood from a high priest to that man's son and the baptism of Jesus in the Jordan River. Describe each aspect of this symbolism on the lines below:

   a. The high priest's son was submerged in water for purification.

   _____

   _____

   b. Holy oil was poured on the head of the high priest's son.

   _____

   _____

   c. The high priest publicly declared that this was his son.

   _____

   _____

2. What is the symbolism in the New Testament example of Caiaphas ripping his garment as Jesus Christ stood before him on the day before Christ's crucifixion?

   _____

   _____

3. What is the symbolism in Christ's final words, "It is finished"?

_____

_____

_____

4. This chapter enlightens us to the fact that with the event of the crucifixion of Christ, our sacrificial lamb, and the ripping of the temple veil top to bottom, God instituted a new priesthood—the priesthood of the believer. Yet today, many traditional churches teach that only a _____ or a _____ can perform a Communion. As "a royal priesthood" (1 Pet. 2:9), we have been given authority to receive the bread and body of Christ. What is it that restrains many from doing so?

   The _____of _____

5. This chapter also compared our human bodies, which are "the temple of God," to the temple in Jerusalem and focused us on the need to be sure our bodies are kept in good repair as the temple of God. We learned of things that can harm our bodies. How do you need to be more diligent about keeping your body—God's temple—in better *repair*? How will you do this?

_____

_____

_____

# CHAPTER 7

# THE GREATEST HINDRANCE TO RECEIVING HEALING

For if ye forgive men their trespasses, your heavenly Father will also forgive you: But if ye forgive not men their trespasses, neither will your Father forgive your trespasses.

—MATTHEW 6:14–15

HAVE YOU EVER PRAYED and felt that the ceiling of the church was a sheet of brass? Has your worship ever felt as though you are speaking into a hollowed log? Or have you ever prayed for a specific need to be met and felt like your words were lost in outer space? Biblically, prayers can be hindered (1 Pet. 3:7), delayed (Dan. 10:11–13), and under some conditions, not heard by the Lord (Mark 11:25). If prayers can be hindered, then so can the manifestation of your healing.

Communication with God (prayer) is the verbal umbilical chord that connects us to God. Under the old covenant, male circumcision sealed the covenant between God and Abraham's seed. The altars were places of sacrifice where God's covenant promises and man's future blessings were sealed with the blood of animals (Gen. 15:1–18). Obedience to God's Word was the key that unlocked the blessings promised by the Lord. God instructed Israel:

> Now therefore, if ye will obey my voice indeed, and keep my covenant, then ye shall be a peculiar treasure unto me above all people: for all the earth is mine.
>
> —EXODUS 19:5

If Israel obeyed God's commandments, He would abundantly prosper and bless them. If they disobeyed, God permitted trouble, distress, and anguish to come upon the nation (Deut. 28). Israel could release the favor of God or hinder the blessings of God by their words and action.

The new covenant was cut with mankind at Christ's crucifixion but was sealed at Christ's resurrection (Heb. 12:24). Circumcision of the male foreskin (Gen. 17:11) was replaced with spiritual circumcision of the heart (Rom. 2:29). The new covenant also requires that conditions be met in order for the blessing of the covenant to be released. Jesus said:

> If you abide in Me, and My words abide in you, you will ask what you desire, and it shall be done for you.
>
> —JOHN 15:7, NKJV

The Greek word for *abide* means, "to stay in a given place; to remain in relation with."[1] All new covenant blessings are based upon an active relationship with Christ, not a mental knowledge of God or an intellectual understanding of certain spiritual concepts, but an inner working of the Holy Spirit that comes through confessing Christ as your Savior and Lord. Some people receive Christ as Savior because they want fire insurance (they want to escape hell), but a true covenant believer will also accept Christ's lordship, meaning, He is the master—the boss, if you please—and you are His obedient servant.

Abiding and being obedient are the power twins of the covenant. If you obey, you will abide; and if you are abiding, you are obeying. Yet the greatest commandment given to new covenant followers is very simple, but at times it is difficult to keep. It is the commandment to walk in continual love. It is easy to love God, but at times it is difficult to love people. Yet Jesus taught this was the greatest commandment:

> A new commandment I give unto you, That you love one another; as I have loved you, that you also love one another. By this shall all men know that ye are my disciples, if ye have love one to another.
>
> —JOHN 13:34–35

In the Bible there are five different Greek words for the English word *love*. Each describes a unique expression of love, and each has a different meaning.

| GREEK WORD | MEANING |
|---|---|
| Agape | To love in a social or moral sense (John 15:10) |
| Phileo | To love as a friend, be fond of, have affection and feeling for (John 21:15) |
| Philadelphia | A fraternal brotherly love and affection for (Rom. 12:10) |
| Philandros | The affection of a man and a wife (Titus 2:4) |
| Philoteknos | The love for one's children (Titus 2:4) |

When our love ceases for our fellow brothers and sisters in Christ, a door is opened for the adversary to work, and the door is closed for God to bless. The greatest hindrance in the body of Christ to walking in love is a spirit of strife, bitterness, and unforgiveness.

## THE GREATEST HINDRANCE

When Christ healed the sick, He often linked forgiveness with the healing. When a paralyzed man was cured at the pool of Bethesda, Christ instructed him to go and sin no more lest a worst thing come upon him (John 5:14). Here, forgiveness, freedom from sin, and healing are linked. Here is another occasion where Christ connected forgiveness and healing:

> Then behold, they brought to Him a paralytic lying on a bed. When Jesus saw their faith, He said to the paralytic, "Son, be of good cheer; your sins are forgiven you." And at once some of the scribes said within themselves, "This Man blasphemes!" But Jesus, knowing their thoughts, said, "Why do you think evil in your hearts? For which is easier, to say, 'Your sins are for-

given you,' or to say, 'Arise and walk'? But that you may know that the Son of Man has power on earth to forgive sins"—then He said to the paralytic, "Arise, take up your bed, and go to your house." And he arose and departed to his house.

—MATTHEW 9:2–7, NKJV

James, when addressing his letter to believers, said;

Is anyone among you sick? Let him call for the elders of the church, and let them pray over him, anointing him with oil in the name of the Lord. And the prayer of faith will save the sick, and the Lord will raise him up. And if he has committed sins, he will be forgiven. Confess your trespasses [faults] to one another, and pray for one another, that you maybe healed.

—JAMES 5:14–15, NKJV

*RECEIVING HEALING*

James instructed believers to confess their faults in order to be healed. The Greek word for *faults* alludes to a "slide, a slip, or a willful or unintentional transgression." To confess and ask forgiveness is the only method established to release a person from sin. The danger is that unforgiveness is not only a sin against a person; it is also a transgression against God. If believers persist in housing an unforgiving spirit in their hearts, Scripture gives strong repercussions that will follow. Understanding this reveals how unforgiveness is the greatest hindrance to receiving healing.

## THE UNFORGIVING SERVANT

Jesus told a parable of a king who had a servant that owed him an amount of money comparable to about fifty-two million dollars. The servant came before the king and begged to be released from his debt. In compassion the king responded to the request, releasing the servant of this burdensome debt.

This servant left the king's presence and found a fellow servant who owed him about fifty-two dollars. The forgiven servant seized the man and demanded that he pay the bill. When the king heard of the inhumane treatment by the man he forgave, he sent his soldiers to arrest the man and place him in prison.

And his master was angry, and delivered him to the torturers until he should
pay all that was due to him.

—MATTHEW 18:34, NKJV

The King James translation says he was turned over to the "tormentors." In
ancient times a prison tormentor was a guard who would beat the prisoner until he
released information or submitted to the will of the king. Imagine this man being
chained in the king's prison and beaten until he repaid his enormous debt. What
a high price to pay for walking in unforgiveness. However, the next statement that
Jesus made is even more shocking:

So likewise shall my heavenly Father do also unto you, if ye from your hearts
forgive not every one his brothers their trespasses.

—MATTHEW 18:35

What exactly does it mean when Jesus said that an unforgiving servant would
be turned over to the tormentor? The apostle Paul's letter to Timothy may help
unlock the warning Christ gave. Timothy was a pastor and had certain elders who
were causing him difficulty because he was a young pastor. Paul wrote:

In humility correcting those who are in opposition, if God perhaps will
grant them repentance, so that they may know the truth, and that they may
come to their senses and escape the snare of the devil, having been taken
captive by him to do his will.

—2 TIMOTHY 2:25–26, NKJV

Strife and confusion are a breeding ground that creates negative feelings
toward others. Those feelings can lead to a root of bitterness that, when matured,
produces the fruit of unforgiveness. Abiding in unforgiveness can give Satan and
his operatives an open door to take the unforgiving servant captive. In this passage,
the Greek word for *captive* means "a prisoner of war or to ensnare."[2]

An example of how a wrong spirit can open the door to a tormenting spirit is
in the life of King Saul. In ancient Israel, Saul was appointed and anointed king.
Because of pride and disobedience, God's Spirit departed from him, and God

raised up David to replace him. After David killed Goliath, he was permitted to marry Saul's daughter and live in the palace. A spirit of jealousy overcame Saul, and he began to physically attack David and attempted to slay him with a spear. The Bible says:

> But the Spirit of the LORD departed from Saul, and a distressing spirit from the LORD troubled him.
>
> —1 SAMUEL 16:14, NKJV

This distressing (evil) spirit is mentioned in three passages (1 Sam. 16:14; 18:10; 19:9). When it overcame Saul, he attempted to kill his opponent, David. The bitterness in Saul's heart opened a door to the enemy in the same manner that an unforgiving spirit will open the door to the adversary.

Jesus made a bold declaration related to unforgiveness when He said:

> For if ye forgive men their trespasses, your heavenly Father will also forgive you: But if ye forgive not men their trespasses, neither will your Father forgive your trespasses.
>
> —MATTHEW 6:14–15

The picture is clear. Our own forgiveness is contingent upon our willingness to forgive those who have offended us. Christ took our sins for us and would not die on the cross until He prayed, "Father, forgive them; for they know not what they do" (Luke 23:34). Christ Himself would not die with unforgiveness in His heart toward His enemies.

When Stephen was being stoned by religious zealots who believed they were doing God a favor in removing the scourge of Christian leaders from Jerusalem, Stephen cried out, "Lay not this sin to their charge" (Acts 7:60). If Jesus could forgive those crucifying Him and Stephen could pray for those murdering him, how much more can we forgive and release people who have offended and wronged us?

If we willfully refuse to forgive, God cannot forgive us. Christ's warning implies that if we pray prayers with unforgiveness, our prayers will be hindered. I believe the same is true with our spiritual warfare. How can a believer resist the enemy

(James 4:7) and attempt to bind the powers of Satan (Matt. 18:18) when the heart is holding grudges toward others in the body of Christ? If God does not hear our prayer, then Satan is not obligated to hear our rebukes!

After more than thirty years of full-time ministry, I believe the greatest hindrance to a believer receiving healing is when unforgiveness blocks his or her spirit. When you do not forgive, you are holding people behind imaginary bars in your mental prison. Christ released you from a spiritual prison and an eternal destination of darkness and death. Yet we tend to take the offenders captive, refusing to talk to people, not fellowshiping with them, and even making negative comments in the presence of others. This is displeasing to God and a roadblock on your road to health and healing.

## REMOVING THE GOAT IN YOUR LIFE

At the temple on the Day of Atonement, when the two goats were offered, the scapegoat was led into the wilderness after the high priest laid hands on the goat's head and transferred Israel's sins onto the goat. Jewish tradition says the goat was led outside of Jerusalem and pushed off a huge cliff, where it plunged to its death. The reason was that Israel did not want the goat to live so that it might wander from the wilderness back into an Israeli community. It would indicate that Israel's sins returned to them once they had been forgiven by God. Once the sins were forgiven, they were never to be brought up again. When Jesus was on the cross and prayed, "Father, forgive them; for they know not what they do," the word *forgive* He used means, "to send forth."[3] In the time of Moses, it would refer to sending forth the scapegoat away from the people on the Day of Atonement. Christ was actually asking God to remit the sins of His enemies in the same manner that the high priest sent the atoning goat into the wilderness of Judea.

After Christ's resurrection He commanded that His disciples be willing to forgive others. He said, "Whose soever sins ye remit, they are remitted unto them; and whose soever sins ye retain, they are retained" (John 20:23). The Greek word for *remit* is the same word as *forgive* that Christ used on the cross. Using the analogy of the scapegoat and the Day of Atonement, Christ was saying that if you forgive a person, then you have removed the goat from your presence and it is now in their house (they are remitted unto them). But if you refuse to forgive, then the sin (old goat) is in your house!

When you live with unforgiveness toward a person, you open a door for the very thing you are criticizing to come upon you. David said it this way:

> Hide me from the secret plots of the wicked,
> From the rebellion of the workers of iniquity,
> Who sharpen their tongue like a sword,
> And bend their bows to shoot their arrows—bitter words,
> That they may shoot in secret at the blameless;
> Suddenly they shoot at him and do not fear.
> They encourage themselves in an evil matter;
> They talk of laying snares secretly;
> They say, "Who will see them?"
> They devise iniquities:
> "We have perfected a shrewd scheme."
> Both the inward thought and the heart of man are deep.
> But God shall shoot at them with an arrow;
> Suddenly they shall be wounded.
> So He will make them stumble over their own tongue.
>
> —PSALM 64:2–8, NKJV

Bitter and angry words are compared to a tongue like a sword and arrows. When a person in secret shoots unfounded and critical words against another person, God says that He will make them stumble on their own tongue and they shall be wounded. As an example, many years ago a noted evangelist was exposed for a moral sin. Most Christians were saddened and hurt. However, another fellow minister spoke out and called the brother a "cancer in Christ's body." Within two years, this man was caught in a similar sin. Perhaps this is what Jesus meant when He said, "Judge not, that you be not judged. For with what judgment you judge,

you will be judged; and with the measure you use, it will be measured back to you"
(Matt. 7:1–2, NKJV).

When we judge a person for their problems, God can permit those bitter arrows
to return to us and remove our own hedge of protection. It seems the Lord allows
us to experience the very things we are criticizing others for! When you are critical of a family whose son is on drugs, your own family hedge may be disrupted by
a child who has a similar problem. One former church member of my father was
outspoken and negative toward a woman in the church whose daughter became
pregnant out of wedlock. Months later the critic was grieved as both of her daughters, who seldom attended church, became pregnant outside of marriage. What she
judged in others came back on her.

## FORGIVENESS AND FREEDOM FROM TEMPTATION

Forgiveness is also linked to freedom from temptation. Matthew 24 lists several
signs that will occur prior to Christ's return. Christ mentioned wars, rumors of
wars, famines, pestilence, and earthquakes (Matt. 24:3–7). Jesus said, "He who
endures to the end shall be saved" (v. 13, NKJV). Was He speaking about enduring
the terrible conflicts and disasters that were coming? I believe that enduring to the
end refers to something more than enduring the stress of the End Times. If you
read the verses just prior to this statement, Christ said:

> And then many will be offended, and will betray one another, and will hate
> one another. Then many false prophets will rise up and deceive many. And
> because lawlessness will abound, the love of many will grow cold. But he
> who endures to the end shall be saved.
> —MATTHEW 24:10–13, NKJV

Jesus revealed that believers will experience offenses prior to His return. The
Greek word for offense is *skandalon*, which means "to set a trap; to entice to do
wrong."[4] When an offense spreads, it can create a church scandal! People gossip,
imaginations run wild, and everyone has an opinion. Rumors breed rumors, and
where there is strife, there is confusion. Soon offended people are "prophesying"

false words to influence others to join their offense. You've heard them say, "The Lord has revealed to me..." as though they are seeing something others aren't. Soon division splits the church, and two groups are offended at each other. The offense grows like a cancer, killing the joy and life in the church. Some people quit attending church and vow never to return again. They have not endured the offense, and they will lose out on God's blessing. More people have left a church because of offense, and more people will miss their healing because of an offended spirit.

Forgiveness is required before you can enjoy emotional, spiritual, and physical healing; forgiveness is also linked to a person's freedom from temptation. We can see this connection in the Lord's Prayer that Christ taught His disciples to pray:

> Our Father in heaven, Hallowed be Your name. Your kingdom come. Your will be done on earth as it is in heaven. Give us this day our daily bread. And forgive us our debts, as we forgive our debtors. And do not lead us into temptation, but deliver us from the evil one. For Yours is the kingdom and the power and the glory forever. Amen.
> —MATTHEW 6:9–13, NKJV

In the parable of the unforgiving servant, the servant owed a debt to the king that was forgiven. Jesus said, "Forgive us our debts, *as* we forgive [release]" the debts of others. We receive this forgiveness *as* we forgive others. Jesus continued, "*And* do not lead us into temptation, but deliver us from the evil one." If unforgiveness can cause a tormentor to come against us, then this tormentor can also create temptations against us. When one minister railed against another minister who was caught in a sexual sin, the accuser succumbed to his own temptation, confessing that he had prayed but could not get delivered from his sexual addiction. I submit to you that he judged another, and the same judgment came to him. He did not forgive and was turned over to a tormenting spirit. He did not release the brother who had fallen, and he himself fell into temptation and was not delivered from the evil one.

We must endure, or maintain our walk under pressure, in order to be victorious in the end. To restrain the tormenting spirit, resist temptation, and live an overcoming life, we must practice forgiveness. This is one reason why daily Communion and receiving the blood and body of Christ is so powerful. Each day we examine our motives, our hearts, and our relationship with God and with man.

## THE POWER OF COMMUNION TO RELEASE

Part of the spiritual self-examination before receiving the Lord's Supper involves the willful choice we make to forgive others as Christ forgave us. His willingness to shed His blood and expose His body to a torturous beating for our atonement is a reminder for us to crucify our own fleshly desires and be willing to take up our own cross and follow His example. He released the guilty, and we must, in our hearts, release the offenses.

When I receive the Lord's Supper, I first give thanks to God for Christ's redemptive work. I then do an inward examination of any actions of disobedience I may have committed in thought, word, or deed. I confess any action and ask God for His forgiveness and cleansing. I proceed to search my heart to sense if there is anyone whom I have an offense or negative feelings toward. This process keeps my body, soul, and spirit clean before God and man.

This process also releases any condemnation that the adversary might place in your mind. There is a difference between *conviction* and *condemnation*. The Bible says the Holy Spirit will reprove you when you sin. *Reprove* means, "to convict; to reprove or strongly admonish." If you sin, the Holy Spirit will convict you with a strong burden and feeling that you did something wrong. That needs to be corrected. Once you confess, repent, and receive forgiveness, the conviction ceases. The enemy, however, will often attempt to bring condemnation, or accuse you with a false verdict. Condemnation is a powerful weapon. This spiritual emotion can destroy your confidence in God's willingness to bless you. Without that confidence, your faith is weakened. Scripture says:

There is therefore now no condemnation to those who are in Christ Jesus, who do not walk according to the flesh, but according to the Spirit.

—ROMANS 8:1–2, NKJV

God wants us free of condemnation.

For if our heart condemns us, God is greater than our heart, and knows all things. Beloved, if our heart does not condemn us, we have confidence toward God. And whatever we ask we receive from Him, because we keep His commandments and do those things that are pleasing in His sight.

—1 JOHN 3:20–23, NKJV

Guilt creates condemnation, but freedom from condemnation produces confidence in our prayers. Through the self-examination of Communion, any sin, guilt, and condemnation will not remain in us. When I understand the admonition to, "Let a man examine himself," then this examination can uncover the areas where the enemy is attempting to gain entrance in our lives. Once I confess my sins, He is "faithful and just to forgive us our sins, and to cleanse us from all unrighteousness" (1 John 1:9).

If we allow bitterness to rule over us, it can literally make us physically sick. Many Christian physicians acknowledge that hospital beds are full of sick people whose biggest problem is not what they are eating, but what is eating them. Let me say it this way: it might not be what they are eating but *whom* they are eating.

## EATING PEOPLE OR FEEDING OFF CHRIST?

The apostle Paul warned the church in Galatians 5:15 not to bite and devour one another. The Greek word for *devour* means "to eat down."[5] We would say they are gnawing on each other, like an animal gnawing at a bone and attempting to extract the last piece of flesh from it. This "eating one another" figuratively referred to speaking against or railing against each other. We would say they were critical of each other. According to Paul, some church members were attempting to force the church back under certain Mosaic laws and were underestimating the grace of God.

The children of Israel exemplified what can occur when people eat the wrong flesh. God sent the people manna, but they lusted after flesh and complained that they wanted meat to eat. God sent a strong wind across the sea and dropped thousands of quail in the camp of the Hebrews. They fell two cubits deep, which translates to thirty-six inches high around the camp. The Bible reveals that the quail fell for two days (Num. 11:31–32). Six hundred thousand men stayed up for about thirty-six hours to collect the fallen birds; "he that gathered least gathered ten homers" (v. 32). According to Dake's Annotated Reference Bible, one homer was ten and one-half bushels, so ten homers would be one hundred five bushels of birds. After gorging themselves with flesh, God smote the people with a plague. They got what they wanted, but they later didn't like what they got!

There is a spiritual parallel for us in this story. You can choose between the heavenly manna and the flesh. You can devour the blood and body of Christ (the bread and fruit of the vine), or you can choose to make a diet of people you don't like, relatives you despise, and folks who have offended you. Just remember that there is life in the manna, the bread from heaven who today is Christ!

> Whoever eats My flesh and drinks My blood has eternal life, and I will raise him up at the last day.
>
> —JOHN 6:54, NKJV

If you have lived with an offense and have allowed unforgiveness to rule your spirit, this will be a hindrance to your spiritual blessings and a stronghold that stops the healing power of God from flowing to you. Jesus said that we should ask for our daily bread. This refers to our provisions for life, but Christ is the bread from heaven. Participating in daily Communion provides us with our daily bread. When we receive the daily bread of the Lord's body, it causes us to examine ourselves, thus keeping our spirit and soul clean and clear.

The manna extended the life of the Hebrews in the wilderness. Your willingness to forgive others and receive the spiritual manna through the Communion can be a vital key to extending your life and strengthening your spirit.

## Four Things to Do

I once heard Pastor Franklin Hunt from Fayetteville, North Carolina, explain the four things a person must do to begin a process of deliverance from bondage and addiction. This same process holds true for receiving deliverance from bitterness and unforgiveness.

1. **Face it.** Do not deny your feelings, and don't blame others for your negative emotions. Face it as a man or woman who loves God. You will never change what you permit and never face what you deny.

2. **Trace it.** Get to the root of your conflict. Was it pride on your part? Did you reject godly advice? Was it the enemy attempting to create a rift? Did you misunderstand someone's comment? Identify the root and deal with that instead of the surface circumstance.

3. **Erase it.** By asking forgiveness, and at times facing the person directly to ask their forgiveness, you are erasing the offense. God will also blot it from any record in heaven and will cleanse it out of your spirit. The enemy may attempt to bring back a memory for a season, but the Holy Spirit will raise up and remind you that you need not remember a sin that God has forgotten!

4. **Replace it.** Old images can be replaced with new pictures. Make fresh memories. Build new relationships. Get on with your life as you leave your past behind.

Get rid of unforgiveness before the seeds of resentment breed a root of bitterness that will choke the blessings of God from your life.

## For Your Reflection

1. In this book we are learning the supernatural power of the "meal that heals" to bring physical and spiritual healing to believers as they

take daily Communion. However, this chapter reveals the greatest
hindrance to healing. What is it?

_____

_____

2. In Matthew 7:1–2, Jesus warned us not to judge, because the very
   thing we are judging another for may become a problem in our own
   lives. Give an example of how this could happen.

_____

_____

_____

3. In the parable of the unforgiving servant (Matt. 18), we are told that
   the servant was "delivered to the torturers until he should pay all
   that was due to him." How does our unforgiveness become an *open
   door* for Satan to ensnare us and become a tormenting spirit in our
   lives?

_____

_____

_____

4. As we submit to self-examination daily as we partake in Communion,
   how can we do each of the following things to ensure that we are
   receiving deliverance from bitterness and unforgiveness?

   a. Face it:

_____

_____

b. Trace it:

_____

_____

c. Erase it:

_____

_____

d. Replace it:

_____

_____

# CHAPTER 8

# COMMUNION—NOT A MAGICAL FORMULA

For this is my blood of the new testament [covenant], which is shed for many for the remission of sins.

—MATTHEW 26:28

SEVERAL YEARS AGO, AFTER I first wrote a book highlighting the concept of receiving daily Communion for physical healing, I received a letter from a woman whose husband had passed away after a battle with cancer. She read the book and forced her husband to receive Communion every day. Within a few weeks he passed away. In her letter to me, she was bitter and upset as she wrote, "It really doesn't work. If there was anything to it, then my husband would not have died." After reading the details of her and her husband's situation, I certainly felt compassion for her. However, I immediately knew what caused the confusion. First was a lack of personal revelation, and second was her perception of Communion.

The message she read in the book was not received as a personal, dynamic revelation for her husband. She forced him to receive Communion based on what she read and not based upon his personal faith. It was similar to someone who reads a book on how to lose weight in ten easy steps, and they give up after step two because they haven't dropped twenty pounds yet. This teaching must move from the printed page and reach into the depths of your spirit to become a quickened revelation that illuminates your spirit and causes great excitement in your soul.

Also, it appeared from her letter that she perceived that receiving Communion was some sort of magical formula. People, especially Americans, love quick fixes, including the latest fads and miracle cures. We purchase workout equipment and get tired just looking at it. We experiment with the latest revolutionary diet that is guaranteed to vanquish love handles. After a few weeks, if we don't melt the pounds like Jell-O in hot water, we assume it doesn't work for us; we just have one of those rare bodies that don't respond properly to the recommended formula.

Two points must be made clear. If a person believes for God to restore his or her health or bring a supernatural healing, then any spiritual method of healing revealed in the Bible must be read through the glasses of faith. In every miracle that Christ performed, the faith of the individual was linked to the manifestation of the miracle. If I read a promise from the Scriptures stating that I can be born again, but I do not believe it, then that promise is automatically void in my life. The same is true if I read about the End-Time outpouring of the Holy Spirit, but believe it is not for our day and time. The Lord does not force His blessings upon anyone. Therefore my unbelief can make void the promises of God for me personally (Matt. 13:58). If an individual reads the promises of healing through the atoning work of Christ and does not believe it, then he will not receive it. Here is what the Bible tells us:

> But without faith it is impossible to please Him, for he who comes to God must believe that He is, and that He is a rewarder of those who diligently seek Him.
>
> —Hebrews 11:6, nkjv

I have personally ministered to hundreds of thousands of individuals during thousands of revivals, conferences, and special services. When ministering in the altar services I have observed the difference between a person who is expecting the Lord to move on his or her behalf and the person who is coming forward just to see what may happen when the prayer is offered. Almost every time, those who have a high level of faith and expectancy are the ones who leave with the blessing. It has been my experience that those who come forward and go through the routine of prayer without much feeling, revelation of the Spirit, or anticipation of an expected result seldom receive a breakthrough at that moment. They often depart the altar, saying, "Just keep praying for me."

When receiving Communion with the emphasis of releasing God's healing anointing into our body, soul, or spirit, we should never simply go through the physical motions with an attitude of, "Let's see if this works." We need to understand Communion in terms of God's covenant with man, since redemption and the cross are the key to unlocking the promises of the new covenant.

## WHAT IS A COVENANT?

Your English translation of the Bible is divided into two sections called the Old and New Testaments. The English word *testament* alludes to a last will and testament, which reveals the benefits left to a family after the death of the testator. Another term is old covenant and new covenant. Since some Christians consider the Old Testament to be outdated and done away with, I prefer to call them the first covenant and the second covenant: the first being the covenant in the Old Testament, and the second being the one initiated with Christ. The sixty-six books of the Bible are a summary of God's covenants with mankind.

The Hebrew word for *covenant* is *berit*, and it speaks of a binding contract between two people. The covenants of God are binding contracts between Him and the person(s) involved. Some of God's covenants include:

| THE COVENANT | THE PROMISE OF THE COVENANT |
|---|---|
| Noachian covenant | The earth would never be destroyed by water again. |
| Abrahamic covenant | Abraham's son would produce a nation and rule the nations. |
| Davidic covenant | David would rule from Jerusalem as king forever. |
| New covenant | We can receive eternal life through Christ. |

Every covenant was, in some way, sealed in blood. In the days after the Flood, Noah burned sacrifices on the altar and God made an agreement that the earth would never be destroyed by water again. In the Abrahamic covenant, the physical act of circumcision was the sign that a Jewish male had "cut the covenant" with God. On the eighth day, every male child was circumcised in the flesh of their foreskin as a token of the Hebrew covenant with God. This was a physical sign that the male child would be raised to believe in the God of Abraham and that he would be raised in a covenant relationship (Gen. 17:11–12).

After the resurrection of Christ and the grafting in of the Gentiles into the church, it was no longer necessary for a believer in Christ to be physically circumcised in his flesh. Paul taught that true circumcision was when God removed the hardness of a person's heart after that person accepted Christ and the new covenant. Under the new covenant, water baptism replaced the physical act of circumcision.

> In whom also ye are circumcised with the circumcision made without hands,
> in putting off the body of the sins of the flesh by the circumcision of Christ:
> Buried with him in baptism, wherein also ye are risen with him through the
> faith of the operation of God, who hath raised him from the dead.
>
> —COLOSSIANS 2:11–12

Under the first covenant, if a Jewish male child was not circumcised the eighth day after his birth, he was not in covenant, and, as an adult, he could be cut off from among the people (Gen. 17:14). Water baptism is so important to the salvation process that Christ taught that people should repent of their sins *and* be baptized. In the Book of Acts, Peter linked repentance and water baptism to the act of salvation (Acts 2:38).

Water baptism identifies you publicly as a believer in Christ. It is a picture of you being buried in Christ and coming up out of the water with a new life. In the early church, baptism immediately followed a person's conversion to Christ (Acts 2:38; 8:12, 38; 9:18; 10:48; 16:15; 18:8; 19:5; 22:16). Water baptism should be emphasized the moment a person comes to Christ.

The act of participation in the Communion meal also identifies you as a believer in Christ.

## THE PRAYER OF FAITH AND THE COMMUNION MEAL

When I began to understand the spiritual truth behind the power of Communion, one of the important areas of illumination was the power of Communion as it relates to faith and healing.

There are many methods of healing found in the Scriptures. There is healing by speaking the Word, healing through a manifestation of the Spirit, healing through the gifts of the Spirit, and healing through the prayer of faith. We are told that the prayer of faith will save the sick and the Lord will raise them up (James 5:15).

During a prayer of faith, the lack of faith (or unbelief) can become a hindrance to the prayer being answered. There are times when a person's faith may be stronger than other times, and we often judge the power of our prayers on the circumstances or feelings surrounding the request. For example, we might think that a migraine headache is no problem for God to heal, but terminal cancer is another story. In many methods of healing, the manifestation comes as a result of the person's faith.

The same is true with Communion. A person must believe in healing power of Christ's body and blood, and that the redemptive anointing of Christ is working in his or her body to produce healing and strength. Faith is the path that all spiritual blessings follow. Communion is powerful because it is based upon God's covenant with us. When I receive Communion, I sense such a relief knowing that I am leaning, not on another person's prayers or another person's faith, but upon simple trust in God's covenant! It takes the human pressure off a person who thinks he or she must have a stronger faith, a special atmosphere, or a greater anointing to see a manifestation of healing.

## HEALING CRUSADES AND CONFERENCES

In the 1940s and 1950s, there were many ministers who operated in the gifts of healing and miracles as spoken of in 1 Corinthians 12:7–10. Multitudes attended these meetings, and many were healed of sicknesses and diseases. My father recalls how people would say, "If I can just get to the big tent revival of Brother So-and-so, I will be healed." Many times they were healed because they released their faith, not in the man, but in the anointing present when he prayed for the sick.

In those days there might be thousands of people attending the service each night. The ministers often sat in chairs and prayed for hours on end for individuals in the prayer line. The ministers would become weary and, if a person was missed in the prayer line, he or she left disappointed. Today there are people who attend healing meetings and leave disappointed because the minister didn't call them out or the Lord didn't seem to have His eye on them. The secular unbeliever often mocks these meetings and considers them a sham or a show. This causes stress on the ministers who walk in this calling, because the sincere ones have a burden for people and are often accused of being a fraud because someone was prayed for who wasn't healed.

One great minister in the 1940s was told by a skeptical preacher, "If you can really heal the sick, go to the local hospital and pray for them to be healed. Empty out the intensive care unit." The man answered, "You are a preacher. Why don't you go to the hospital and win them all to the Lord? Get everyone saved if you believe in salvation." The skeptic replied, "A person must believe in order to be saved." The healing minister replied, "And a person must believe in order to be healed!"

Others seeking healing often believe there must be a certain atmosphere created to ensure the healing prayer has worked. Even some ministers cannot operate under an "anointing" unless the stage, the music, and the lighting are set just right.

God does use people to minister to others, and He does bring special miracles through the anointing of His Spirit (Acts 19:11). However, I believe the most perfect way of receiving anything from the Lord is through your *own personal faith* in the Word. This is why Communion is so powerful. God is true to His covenant. He is true to His Word. He has magnified His Word above His name (Ps. 138:2). God is so true to His covenant that when He threatened to destroy the Hebrews for worshiping the golden calf, Moses simply reminded God of His covenant with Abraham. With that reminder, the Lord repented of His decision to destroy Israel (Exod. 32:14).

## ACTING OUT YOUR FAITH

Faith without works (action) is dead (James 2:26). Often before Christ healed the sick, He asked the person to perform an act of faith to demonstrate that the person believed for his miracle. For example, Jesus said:

- "Stretch forth thy hand," to a man with a withered hand (Luke 6:10)
- "Go, and shew thyself to the priests," to ten lepers (Luke 5:14)
- "Rise, take up thy bed, and walk," to a paralyzed man (John 5:8)
- "Go, wash in the pool of Siloam," to a blind man (John 9:7)

Years ago a gifted evangelist had great results ministering to the sick. Before prayer he would tell folks to act out their faith by doing what they could do; for example, to move a part of their body or to begin praising God in advance. A young girl had been involved in an accident and was paralyzed from the neck down. She began moving her eyes up and down as a sign of her faith that God would heal her. The minister knew what she was doing; she was acting on her faith in the only manner she could—by moving the only thing she could move, her eyes. As he prayed for her, the power of God rushed through her body, and she was able to stand up and walk. Her mother was so shocked that she fainted!

By taking the time to prepare the Communion supper and spend time meditating on Christ and His covenant, you are acting on your faith. You would not take time to go through the process if you did not consider Communion an act of great importance in your life. God loves to see people act out their faith, and He loves it when we understand His covenant. The Bible says:

> My covenant will I not break, nor alter the thing that is gone out of my lips.
> —PSALM 89:34

## RELYING ON GOD'S PROMISES

The Old Testament was based upon obedience to the written law of God recorded in the five books of Moses called the Torah. The new covenant is based upon walking in repentance and forgiveness and acting upon the promises given in the New Testament. Paul taught that we have a better covenant established on better promises (Heb. 8:6). By definition, a promise is a divine assurance of something good. Below are a few of the many promises given to believers in the New Testament:

- Salvation by faith (Eph. 2:8)
- Justification by faith (Rom. 5:1)
- The promise of the Holy Spirit (Acts 2:39)
- The promise of healing (1 Pet. 2:24)
- The promise of Christ's return (Acts 1:11)
- The promise of heaven (John 14:2–3)
- The promise of eternal life (John 3:14–17)
- The promise of ruling with Christ (Rev. 20:6)

Receiving Communion is both an act of faith and an act of obedience. God is moved toward us when He sees us act upon our faith in His Word and believe the words of His covenant. Jesus said it this way:

> If ye abide in me, and my words abide in you, ye shall ask what ye will, and it shall be done unto you.
>
> —JOHN 15:7

## FOR YOUR REFLECTION

1. This chapter reveals the powerful spiritual connection between daily observance of Communion and healing. In your own words, describe how this observance can strengthen our faith for healing.

_____

_____

_____

2. We also learned in this chapter that God is always true to His Word and to the covenants He has made with His people. What two biblical characters exercised great faith by reminding God about a covenant He had made that resulted in God withholding a judgment He had made?

_____

_____

_____

3. It is very important for God's people to act out their faith for a miracle. In each of the following scriptures, a person demonstrated faith in a promised healing. Briefly describe each event:

   a. Luke 6:10

_____

_____

   b. Luke 5:14

_____

_____

    c.   John 5:8

_____

_____

    d.   John 9:7

_____

_____

4.   God's Word is filled with His promises. On the lines below, name one promise God has made that has been particularly "faith building" for you, and explain why it has been so important.

_____

_____

_____

_____

CHAPTER 9

# WHEN SICKNESS TRIES TO RETURN TO YOUR HOUSE

When an unclean spirit goes out of a man, he goes through dry places, seeking rest; and finding none, he says, "I will return to my house from which I came." And when he comes, he finds it swept and put in order. Then he goes and takes with him seven other spirits more wicked than himself, and they enter and dwell there; and the last state of that man is worse than the first.

—LUKE 11:24–26, NKJV

WHILE THE PROMISES OF the new covenant are free, seeing them manifest in your life is a battle—a battle that involves your faith. The enemy will throw mental darts such as: Is it really God's will that I be healed? Is God trying to teach me a lesson? Is this problem a result of some sin? Many believers struggle to receive because they are continually bombarded with negative messages from the enemy of their soul. One of the most challenging and difficult conflicts will manifest when the enemy attempts to return to your house.

Luke recorded the statement by Jesus that the unclean spirit departs but attempts to return to the same house from where it was expelled. Notice that the house is swept and garnished, but it is uninhabited. The person in this story has made an effort to "straighten up" and has received temporary relief, but he has not properly allowed the Lord to move in and take up residence. Eventually, the enemy moved back in and brought some unwanted company (seven other spirits) with him.

In Mark chapter 5, when Christ delivered the man of Gadara from two thousand unclean spirits (v. 13), this former maniac from the mountains wanted to follow Jesus from city to city. Christ told this former demon-possessed man to go home and tell his friends what great things the Lord had done for him (v. 19). Instead of Christ encouraging the man to follow Him, He told the man to return to where he came from and testify of his miracle. I believe this man had a slight fear of returning—a fear that the demons would once against attempt to enter him. Jesus gave him a powerful key to staying free. He said, "Testify of what the Lord has done!" This agrees with a statement in Revelation 12:11: "They overcame him [Satan] by the blood of the Lamb and by the word of their testimony."

A born-again believer who is under the covenant of Christ's blood and walking in the Word has a defense against the powers of darkness, including evil spirits. However, there is a spiritual principle that a believer should be made aware of. There are two types of conflicts: attacks and counterattacks. Most Christians are fully aware of a frontal assault from the adversary. However, many are caught off guard when a counterattack comes. The purpose of the enemy's counterattack is to regain lost territory.

When a person becomes born again, the adversary may bring an old B.C. (before Christ) friend who will tempt you to return to the late-night parties and bars. Believers who receive the Holy Spirit baptism often must deal with skeptical relatives who attempt to rescue them from their "deception." The same is true with healing. The early full-gospel ministers were continually defending the practice of praying for the sick as critics bemoaned or denounced the act of anointing with oil and seeking God for healing.

The adversary is a thief and a robber. He dislikes losing ground and therefore will make an attempt to steal your blessing, if you permit him to do so.

## WHEN A SICKNESS RETURNS

For many years my father has prayed for the sick and seen countless answers to prayer. Dad and I have both observed over the years that some people who are healed have at times experienced a relapse of a similar affliction. For example, a person who is healed of a terminal illness is declared clean by their physician. Many years later, the disease returns, but perhaps to another location in their body. While this certainly does not happen all the time, it does happen from time to time and should be addressed.

Once we have been healed, we must maintain our faith in Christ's ability to preserve our whole body, soul, and spirit blameless unto the coming of the Lord Jesus Christ (1 Thess. 5:23). In the 1950s, a woman with cancer on her face was standing for prayer while the evangelist was fervently praying for God to perform miracles. Her hand was covering the large cancer, and she suddenly cried out as the cancer fell into her hand and her face was completely healed. People began rejoicing. The woman, however, said, "I can't believe this…this is impossible…this can't be happening." She placed her hand back to her face, and the cancer melted back into her skin! In shock she made a profound statement, "O God; what my faith took off, my unbelief put back on!"[1]

## DEALING WITH GOLIATH'S BROTHER

The story of Goliath contains a clue as to how to deal with a sickness when it returns. In David's time, there were five giants who lived in the Promised Land. Their names were:

1.   Goliath  (1 Sam. 17:4)
2.   Ishbi-Benob (2 Sam. 21:16)
3.   Saph (2 Sam. 21:18)
4.   The giant from Gath (2 Sam. 21:20)
5.   Lahmi (1 Chron. 20:5)

Goliath was so large and intimidating that no man in the army of Israel was willing to challenge him until a faith-filled teenager arrived on the battlefield. Before approaching Goliath, David stopped by a brook of water and picked up five smooth stones for his slingshot (1 Sam. 17:40). The obvious reason for the five stones was that David was prepared to take out Goliath and his four other colleagues.

Lahmi, one of the four giants, was also a brother to Goliath:

Again there was war with the Philistines, and Elhanan the son of Jair killed Lahmi the brother of Goliath the Gittite, the shaft of whose spear was like a weaver's beam.

—1 Chronicles 20:5, nkjv

If Lahmi was part of the Goliath family, he may have been the same height and had the same facial features and threatening voice of his brother, Goliath. Yet he was not Goliath, because Goliath was dead (1 Sam. 17:51). The very head of Goliath had been removed by the sword of David, a picture of the sword of the Spirit, or the Word of God getting to the root of the problem that is afflicting us (Heb. 4:12).

Once God has wrought a healing for you, whether through the prayer of faith, a manifestation of the Spirit, or through Communion, He makes good His healing work, and your faith and obedience maintain a continual flow of life into your spirit, soul, and body. However, occasionally the enemy will counterattack, attempting to bring the very thing you were freed from back into your body. This is not Goliath, because that giant is dead. It may look the same, feel the same, and act the same, but Goliath has a brother. Lahmi must be dealt with just as Goliath was dealt with.

Many years ago a person came to me asking for prayer. He mentioned that a pervious ailment was attempting to return. I told him, "It's not Goliath; it's his brother. But there are still stones in the brook!" The point was that the same faith that defeated Goliath will also defeat his brother. The same anointing that brought the initial healing and the same faith that defeated the adversary years ago are the same anointing and faith that can conquer the enemy today!

Obviously, if the Lord tarries, we will all have our final day on Earth and pass from this life to the next. We are not presently in an immortal body, and our body, which is the temple of the Holy Spirit (1 Cor. 3:16), requires occasional repairs and maintenance. Throughout our journey storms will come and damage parts of our temple. But just as God cared for His house in Jerusalem, He is concerned about your physical house, which was created in His image.

Here are three points to remember:

1.  God is able to keep (preserve) what we commit to Him, and this includes our health.

Now may the God of peace Himself sanctify you completely; and may your whole spirit, soul, and body be preserved blameless at the coming of our Lord Jesus Christ.

—1 THESSALONIANS 5:23–24, NKJV

2.  If the enemy returns, use the same weapons to defeat him again and again.

For the weapons of our warfare are not carnal but mighty in God for pulling down strongholds.

—2 CORINTHIANS 10:4, NKJV

3.  We should maintain our faith and fellowship through Communion as often as we can or feel led.

In the same manner He also took the cup after supper, saying, "This cup is the new covenant in my blood. This do, as often as you drink it, in remembrance of Me."

—1 CORINTHIANS 11:25, NKJV

## FOR YOUR REFLECTION

1.  Luke chapter 11 tells the story of an unclean spirit leaving a house and then returning with seven more wicked spirits to once again take up residence in the house. What did you learn in this chapter about why Satan often tries to attack us with a disease or illness from which God has already healed us?

_____

_____

_____

2.  This chapter describes two kinds of Satanic attacks—a frontal attack and a counterattack. What is the purpose of a counterattack?

    _____

    _____

    _____

3.  An interesting connection was made between the giant Goliath and the five smooth stones that David picked up to use in his fight with Goliath. What do the other four stones represent?

    _____

    _____

    _____

4.  What are the three important lessons we learned to avoid a counterattack in this chapter?

    a. _____

    _____

    b. _____

    _____

    c. _____

    _____

# CHAPTER 10

# THE SECRET POWER OF THE BLOOD OF THE LAMB

For the life of the flesh is in the blood.

—LEVITICUS 17:11

THIS NIGHT WOULD GO down forever in history. As darkness settled across Egypt, the Hebrew people were roasting lamb, sprinkling blood on their doorposts, and preparing for a visitation from God. Tonight God would send the tenth plague, the death of all the firstborn cattle and firstborn sons of the Egyptians. Only the homes marked by the lamb's blood would be passed over.

God sent ten plagues against Egypt. These plagues were an attack against ten major gods of the Egyptians. For example, Ra was the Egyptian god of the sun, who was powerless when darkness covered the land (Exod. 10:22). Apis was a god shaped like a bull. However, Apis could not prevent the Almighty's judgment on the cattle in Egypt (Exod. 9:6). When the Nile turned to blood (Exod. 7:20), the Egyptian crocodile god was helpless to intervene.

Two chief gods of the Egyptians were named Amon and Khnum. The god Khnum had a human body and a ram's head. He was lord of the first cataract and presided over the annual rise of the Nile, which emerged from two caverns in Elephantine. Egyptians believed that this idol controlled the water, half of which flowed north and half south. When the Nile turned to blood (Exod. 7:20) and the Almighty smote the river with frogs (Exod. 8:3), all the prayers to the stone idol Khnum were useless.

## EGYPTIANS HATED SHEPHERDS

According to Joseph's statements to his brothers, the Egyptians despised shepherds. (See Genesis 46:34.) When Jacob moved the Hebrews to Egypt, Joseph told his brothers not to say they were shepherds, for fear that the Egyptians would not allow the Hebrews to move from Canaan to Egypt.

> So it shall be, when Pharaoh calls you and says, "What is your occupation?" that you shall say, "Your servants' occupation has been with livestock from our youth even till now, both we and also our fathers," that you may dwell in the land of Goshen; for every shepherd is an abomination to the Egyptians.
>
> —GENESIS 46:33–34, NKJV

How ironic that the Egyptians hated shepherds, and yet, God used the lesser and despised animal of a lamb to defeat and destroy the entire nation! The lamb's blood on the door of the Israelites' homes was contempt for these two idol gods.

## SATAN'S TWO STRONGEST FORCES

Just as these two gods were the chief idols in Egypt, Satan had control of the power of sin and sickness. God used the blood of a little lamb to defeat Satan's two strongest agents. This Passover was a future of what would come.

+ This lamb was called a Passover lamb; Jesus was called the Lamb of God.
+ The Exodus lamb was without blemish; Jesus was called sinless or spotless.
+ The lamb's body provided healing; Christ's stripes on His body provide healing.
+ The lamb's blood provided redemption; Christ's blood provides redemption.

It was important for the Israelites to remain in the house as the destroying angel passed by:

> Now the blood shall be a sign for you on the houses where you are. And when I see the blood, I will pass over you; and the plague shall not be on you to destroy you when I strike the land of Egypt.
>
> —EXODUS 12:13, NKJV

> And you shall take a bunch of hyssop, dip it in the blood that is in the basin, and strike the lintel and the two doorposts with the blood that is in the basin. And none of you shall go out of the door of his house until morning.
>
> —EXODUS 12:22, NKJV

Just as the people were required to remain in the house for God's protection, we are to abide in Christ and remain faithful to Him to receive the full benefit of the new covenant.

## THE MYSTERY OF THE BLOOD

How can a small lamb's blood have such authority over death? How can the blood of one man, Jesus Christ, have such power over the enemy? What is so special about the blood?

When God created man in His own image, He breathed into man's nostrils the breath of life and Adam became a living soul (Gen. 2:7). The Hebrew word for *life* is plural, meaning lives. This is because the "life of the flesh is in the blood" (Lev. 17:11) and all the DNA for future generations is in the blood of the father. Many future "lives" are found in the bloodline of just one man.

When God created blood for Adam's body, He placed a life substance that Satan and the angels were not familiar with. Angels are spirits without physical bodies, and man is a spirit being with a physical body. The angels had never known of blood until the creation of Adam. There is also the unusual passage where Cain killed his brother Abel, and the "voice of [Abel's] blood [cried out]…from the ground" (Gen. 4:10). The Hebrew word for *blood* in this passage is *dam*, which is plural.[1] When Cain murdered Abel, he killed not only his brother but also every child and descendant who would in the future come out of Abel's loins. Blood has a voice—an ability to speak to God. Speaking of Abel, the writer to the Hebrews said, "He being dead yet speaketh" (Heb. 11:4).

Without blood you would instantly die. All nourishment for your body comes through your blood, and most diseases can be traced through blood tests. This mysterious liquid was God's gift of life to mankind. It was so important that when sin originated in the garden, it required blood to cover man's sins.

...and without shedding of blood there is no remission.

—HEBREWS 9:22, NKJV

## WHY ALL THE ANIMALS?

When the tabernacle and the temple were constructed, continual sacrifices were offered. Some were sin offerings, others were transgression offerings, and others were offerings of thanksgiving. Only the priest could offer the animals, and only the priest could catch the blood in gold and silver vessels. The atoning blood was sprinkled on the sacred vessels and upon the altar (Lev. 3:2), before the veil (Lev. 4:6), and before the ark and the mercy seat on the Day of Atonement (Lev. 16:15). Human and animal blood could not mix. If a priest accidentally cut himself, he would exit the temple through a special escape route to keep from mingling the blood.

After Adam and Eve's confession of sin, God slew two animals and covered the first couple with the fresh skins of the slain animals. From that moment certain animals were marked for sacrificial offerings. Each animal in some manner would serve as a picture of the ultimate sacrifice of Christ.

The amount of blood was astonishing. The blood of three oxen could fill up a modern bathtub. Consider the following. In Egypt there were 600,000 Hebrew men. If there were 4 men in each house, there could be up to 150,000 lambs offered the night of Passover. In the days of Moses's tabernacle, a lamb was offered in both the morning and the evening for forty years. This would total 28,800 lambs.

In the time of Solomon's temple, the fellowship offering consisted of 22,000 cattle; 120,000 sheep; and 120,000 goats. This would be 262,000 animals with over 290,000 gallons of blood on the altar. When Solomon offered 10,000 sheep, he placed 10,835 gallons of blood on the altar. King Hezekiah sacrificed over 10,000 sheep, and each Passover in Jerusalem there were as high as 300,000 lambs a year, bringing 310,000 gallons of blood a year on the altar of the Lord.[2]

After fifteen hundred years of endless and countless blood offerings, the final Lamb was offered in Jerusalem. Christ was conceived of the Holy Spirit and born of a virgin. Since the blood type of a child comes from the father's seed, Christ's blood would not have been linked to His earthly father, Joseph, but it was directly connected to God Himself. The same original blood in the first Adam, breathed into Him by His creator, was also breathed into Mary's womb, into the body of Christ. Christ's blood was never tainted by Adam's original sin. Christ was sinless and perfect. This is why it took His blood to redeem mankind.

## THE HILL OF A SKULL

The concept of Christ being the Lamb was a fulfillment of the events of Passover. However, there is a lesser-known aspect of His redemptive plan. It concerns the location of Christ's crucifixion. John's Gospel says:

> And He, bearing His cross, went out to a place called the Place of a Skull, which is called in Hebrew, Golgotha, where they crucified Him, and two others with Him, one on either side, and Jesus in the center.
>
> —JOHN 19:17–18, NKJV

In Jerusalem, there are several mountains surrounding the old city of Jerusalem. They are:

+ Mount of Olives
+ Mount Scopus
+ Mount of Evil Council
+ Mount Calvary

+ Mount Moriah
+ Mount Zion
+ Mount Ophel

The Mount of Olives is the most famous mountain in the Old Testament, but Golgotha is the most famous in the New Testament. The Gospel writers name the hill where Christ was led away to be crucified. At that time in Jerusalem, three languages were spoken: Greek, Latin, and Hebrew. For this reason, Pilate placed an inscription on the cross, "Jesus of Nazareth the King of the Jews," in all three languages. The site of the execution was on a hill called Calvary (in Latin) or Golgotha (in Hebrew). The Gospel writers reveal the name of the hill and also one strange fact: it was the hill of a skull. The statement "hill of a skull" has created much speculation about the meaning of that phrase. Whose skull? Why was this area called the place of a skull?

Traditionally, there are three possible explanations. The first tradition dates back through Jewish history and is briefly mentioned by the early father Origen. Jewish legend teaches that prior to the Flood, righteous Noah took the skull of Adam (which would have been over seven hundred years old) and placed it in the ark. Legend states that after the Flood, Noah's son Shem, who would later gain the title Melchizedek, the king and priest of Jerusalem (Gen. 14), buried the skull of Adam in Jerusalem. Thus Origen believed that the name Golgotha alluded to Adam's skull being buried in the same location where the Lord was crucified.[3]

The second tradition is linked to the idea of an ancient stoning ground. Christ was crucified and buried outside of the city gate, since burial tombs were not to be located with the walls of the Holy City. It is believed that the ancient stoning ground was located north of the city, just outside the present Damascus Gate. The first martyr in Jerusalem was Stephen, a deacon in the early church (Acts 7). This godly man was stoned to death at a stoning ground outside the gate of the city. Some suggest that the hill of a skull would refer to the bones of the victims who were stoned. The two negatives of this theory are:

1.    The hill is a hill of *a* skull and not the hill of *skulls* (plural).

2.  There were new tombs and a garden where Christ was crucified. A stoning ground would unlikely have a garden or be near the burial place of a member of the Sanhedrin, such as Joseph of Arimathea. Christ was placed in his tomb after His death.

A third theory, which became popular in the late 1800s, is linked with a small hill presently located at the base of a noisy Arab bus station just outside the Damascus Gate in Jerusalem. In the late 1800s, a British general named Gordon was visiting Jerusalem when he noticed a hill that appeared to have eye sockets, similar to a large skull. He suspected this was the hill of the Crucifixion. Archeological excavations unearthed evidence of an ancient tomb, as well as evidence of a garden located very close to the hill itself. Gordon noted where Scripture mentioned that the place where Christ was crucified had a garden and, in the garden, a new tomb.

Scripture placed the tomb and the garden in the same vicinity of the hill of the skull. In Jerusalem, the traditional site of the crucifixion is called the Church of the Holy Sepulture. This location dates back to the time of Helena, Emperor Constantine's mother who traveled throughout the Holy Land attempting to mark the actual holy sites connected to the ministry of Christ. There is a controversy over this location, because it may actually be located inside of the walls of the old city, which would immediately eliminate it from the true location. Nobody could be crucified or buried within the walls of the city. To do so would defile the sanctity of Jerusalem.

So why was the hill identified as the hill of a skull? Was it linked to the first man Adam? With Christ being the second man Adam, was it necessary that the blood of the cross drip from the old rugged cross into the ground where the bones of the first man was buried? This theory was propagated by an early father named Jerome, who suggested that, during the earthquake at the crucifixion, the blood of Christ dripped from the cross into a crack in the ground and fell on Adam's skull.[4] This sounds dramatic and very spiritual. However, it would take a huge amount of blood to drip deep into the ground and cover a skull that was buried there eighteen hundred years before the crucifixion.

## THE POSSIBLE INTERPRETATION

To understand the probable meaning of Golgotha, one must go back to the time of Noah when a strange race of giants once roamed the earth. When Moses reported the days of Noah, he indicated that there were giants on the earth in those days. Moses further revealed that these giants were the offspring of the sons of God coming into the daughters of men, who bore these mighty men of renown. According to numerous Jewish and early church sources, the giants were born when angels were sent down from God in the form of humans to teach men righteousness and reveal the mysteries of God. Some, however, became enamored with the virgin daughters of men, fell into lust, and had physical relations that birthed an oversized person, often with a height of nine to fifteen feet high.

According to Scriptures, there was once a race of beings called giants who roamed and even ruled parts of the earth. They existed prior to the Flood and were present in the time of David.

This race of giants perverted the earth before the Flood. They caused fear in the Hebrews who desired to enter the Promised Land, and they controlled mountains in Hebron when Joshua and Caleb led Israel into their inheritance (Josh. 15). By the time of David, the last five giants in biblical record were living in Israel. They are listed in 1 Samuel 17:4; 2 Samuel 21:16–22; and 1 Chronicles 20:5. Their names are:

+ Goliath
+ Saph
+ Lahmi
+ Ishbi-Benob
+ The giant from Gath

As a teenager, David slew Goliath and used the giant's own sword to cut off his head:

Therefore David ran, and stood upon the Philistine, and took his sword, and drew it out of the sheath thereof, and slew him, and cut off his head therewith. And when the Philistines saw their champion was dead, they fled.

—1 SAMUEL 17:51

After that verse are the most interesting and overlooked portions of Scripture in the story of David and Goliath. When happened to the head of the giant? The Bible reveals what David did after he defeated the high Philistine champion:

And David took the head of the Philistine, and brought it to Jerusalem; but he put his armor in his tent.

—1 SAMUEL 17:54

What makes this statement unique are the following:

1.  The Philistines were in the Valley of Elah, and Jerusalem is about eighteen miles from this area. David carried the head of the giant over eighteen miles to Jerusalem. Why did David travel so far with the head of his enemy?

2.  At that time Jerusalem was controlled by a Canaanite tribe called the Jebusites. Years later when David became king, he captured the city of Jebus. Why did young David take the skull of Goliath to Jerusalem, when at the time Hebron was considered the capital of Israel?

3.  David took the armor of Goliath and put it in his tent. Which tent was this? He lived in Bethlehem at the time and later built a tent on Mount Zion to worship God. We read where the sword of Goliath was in the tabernacle of Moses at Nob, wrapped in a cloth behind the ephod:

And the priest said, The sword of Goliath the Philistine, whom thou slewest in the valley of Elah, behold, it is here wrapped in a cloth behind the ephod:

if thou wilt take that, take it: for there is no other save that here. And David said, There is none like that; give it me.

—1 SAMUEL 21:9

Did David also place the armor of the giant in the tabernacle along with the giant's sword? Is this the tent the Bible is referring to, or was it a personal tent David was living in? Since the Jebusites controlled Jerusalem and were enemies of Israel, did David take the head immediately, or was the Bible indicating something David did at a later period, after he became king of Israel? We know that David was aware of the story of Abraham, Isaac, and Melchizedek. He had the Torah (first five books in the Bible) and was aware of Abraham's prediction concerning Mount Moriah in Jerusalem, that, "In the mount of the LORD it shall be seen" (Gen. 22:14). David is identified as a prophet in the New Testament (Acts 2:29–30). Peter stated that David saw a preview of the resurrection of Christ (Acts 2:30–31); therefore, he gave various predictions related to this future event.

Apparently, the Holy Spirit inspired David to take the skull of Goliath to Jerusalem, understanding that this giant represented the seed of the serpent (Gen. 3:15) and his defeat represented triumph over all of Israel's enemies. The skull would have been buried in Jerusalem as a reminder that God was with David and had promised him a kingdom there in the future. The fact that David constructed a tent and set up continual worship is significant. The sword of Goliath was wrapped in a cloth in the tabernacle of Moses and placed near the ephod. The linen ephod is what the priest wore when ministering. Years later, after defeating Goliath, David led a procession of priests bearing the ark of the covenant into Jerusalem wearing the special ephod!

And David danced before the LORD with all his might; and David was girded with a linen ephod.

—2 SAMUEL 6:14

## GOLIATH AND GOLGOTHA

The meaning of Golgotha being the hill of a skull could be linked to Adam, but more likely it is linked to Goliath. I believe it is possible that David took the head of the giant to Jerusalem and buried in at a certain hill that would be recognized as skull hill. Centuries of history caused the original meaning and intent of this hill to be lost, but the clues are still hidden in the word Golgotha.

We read in the Bible that Goliath was from Gath. He would have been identified as Goliath of Gath, just as Jesus was known as Jesus of Nazareth and Saul as Saul of Tarsus. A person was often identified with the area where he was from.

Goliath from Gath could be abbreviated to read Gol–Gath–ha! Thus the word *Golgotha* alluded to a skull—a very famous skull that was buried at the base of a hill later named in Hebrew the hill of Golgotha! If this theory is correct, it adds another dynamic dimension to the purpose of Christ being crucified at the hill of a skull!

Here is the picture. As Christ is hanging from the cross on the top of the hill of a skull, His blood is falling on the ground, perhaps in the very area when the skull of the ancient enemy of Israel is buried. Christ's feet were over the head of the enemy. Just as God predicted, the seed of the woman will bruise his (the enemy's) head (Gen. 3:15). The Hebrew word for *bruise* means "to overwhelm, to break, and to cover."[5] As Christ the Lamb was slain near Passover, it appeared that Satan had won. However, Christ broke the power of sin and death and sickness, and put His enemies under His feet!

After Satan's defeat by Christ, we can now proclaim as Paul did to the believers in Rome:

> And the God of peace shall bruise Satan under your feet shortly. The grace of our Lord Jesus Christ be with you. Amen.
>
> —ROMANS 16:20

## For Your Reflection

1. What are the two strongest agents Satan uses to defeat God's people?

   _____

   _____

2. Why is it important for us to understand what is meant in Scripture when it says, "The life of the flesh is in the blood" (Lev. 17:11)?

   _____

   _____

3. This chapter reveals three Jewish traditional schools of thought that attempt to explain why the Bible mentions Christ's crucifixion as taking place on the "place of the skull" (John 19:17–18). Briefly describe each of these theories:

   a. _____

   _____

   b. _____

   _____

   c. _____

   _____

4. The chapter reveals a much different explanation related to the "place of the skull." How might this be related to David's slaying of Goliath?

   _____

   _____

# CHAPTER 11

# THE DIDACHE AND THE MESSIANIC BANQUET

And he saith unto me, Write, Blessed are they which are called unto the marriage supper of the Lamb. And he saith unto me, These are the true sayings of God.

—REVELATION 19:9

BETHLEHEM WAS ONE OF the smallest communities in Israel. Yet, the people born and living in this town affected Israel, and one man born there changed the world. The word *Bethlehem* comes from two Hebrew words: *beyth*, meaning house, and *lechem*, meaning bread. The meaning of Bethlehem is the "house of bread." The prophetic meaning of this town was both literal and spiritual.

The love story of Ruth and Boaz unfolded in Bethlehem. Ruth was a Moabite (Gentile) who followed her Jewish mother-in-law, Naomi, from Moab back to Naomi's home city of Bethlehem at the conclusion of a famine. Ruth, a widow, was permitted to collect barley in the fields of a rich Jew named Boaz. Ruth gained the attention and favor of the rich, single landowner and eventually married him. From the bloodline of Ruth and Boaz came the first prominent citizen of Bethlehem, King David (Ruth 4:21–22).

At the death of Boaz, his son Obed would have inherited his fields. After Obed's death the land was passed to his son Jesse, who was the father of David. These fields grew both barley and wheat, and, during the time of the Jewish temple, the grain from the fields of Bethlehem was harvested and used to make bread at the temple, including the bread baked for the table of showbread. Centuries later, in a stable, the true bread from heaven arrived on the scene in the town of Bethlehem.

Bethlehem was special as far back as the time of Jacob. His wife Rachel died and was buried near Bethlehem after giving birth to their son Benjamin (Gen. 35:17–19). In the time of Joshua, the tribe of Judah was given several cities within their territory, including Bethlehem (Josh. 19:15). Bethlehem was also the village from where the prophet Micah predicted the Ruler of Israel would come. This was understood when, four hundred years later, the wise men arrived in Jerusalem and inquired among Jewish scholars about the place where the King was to be born. Their answer was Bethlehem (Matt. 2:1–6).

Bethlehem is located at the edge of the Judean wilderness. When departing Bethlehem and crossing the barren wilderness toward the Dead Sea, you will eventually come to the ruins of a village that once existed in the time of Christ, called Qumran. In the time of Christ, a mysterious group of men called the Essenes lived and studied in this desert community. According to scholars, this group had a detailed understanding of the community meal.

## THE SPECIAL MEALS AMONG THE JEWS

Some scholars believe that the concept of a "communal meal" may have originated with the Essenes. This secluded group of men is today noted for preserving the famous Dead Sea Scrolls in jars and hiding them in caves for future generations to recover. They were a mystical group who believed in the future redemption of Israel and a Messiah who would arrive and redeem the nation from her enemies.

According to scholars, the Essenes would wash in water, put on white garments, and gather in their assembly hall. They would bless the bread and then the wine. The wine was "young sweet wine before it was fermented." The same blessing procedure is followed in our Communion meal. Believers assemble together, having been cleansed of their sins and given white garments (which represent the righteousness of the saints), and they bless the bread and the fruit of the vine. Washing in a *mik'vot* (similar to an outdoor baptistery) was an important ritual among the men in the community. It is interesting that Jesus washed the feet of His disciples following His final supper (John 13:4–15).

In the first century there was also a group of Egyptian Jewish ascetics called Therapeutae (Greek for healers). They settled near Alexandria in Egypt and lived a life of separation similar to the Essenes. The ancient writer Philo wrote about this group. They spent most of their time in prayer and study, and they read only the Torah, the prophets, and Psalms. For six days they lived in solitude, never leaving the house. On the seventh day, both the men and women met in a double divided sanctuary where they ate a special meal consisting of spring water and bread flavored with hyssop or salt. The group avoided wine and meat. Following the meal, a sacred vigil continued until dawn.[1] Some scholars believe this group of was a branch from the Essenes in a pre-Christian era.

The Essenes' meal was considered a preview of the final meal to be eaten with the Messiah at the end of days. According to the New Testament writers, the Communion meal is closely connected to the Passover meal, called the Seder, which is conducted by the Jews each year to remind them of their deliverance from Egyptian bondage.

Scripture teaches that the Communion supper shows forth the Lord's death until He comes (1 Cor. 11:26). At the final Passover meal, Jesus took the fourth cup, which is called the cup of consummation, and introduced it as the "cup of the kingdom." After all, when He returns for the church and resurrects the dead in Christ, He will transport us into the heavenly kingdom where we will participate in the Marriage Supper of the Lamb, and Christ will consummate the marriage with His bride (Rev. 19:7–9). At the Last Supper Jesus held up this cup and announced that He would not drink it again until He drank it with His followers in the kingdom (Mark 14:25). This was the last Passover meal He ate with His disciples. Believers, however, are reminded of their future meal called the Marriage Supper every time we eat the bread and drink from the cup.

## CORIANDER SEED

The manna in the wilderness was like a coriander seed and was white in color (Num. 11:7). This photo shows coriander seeds painted white, giving a visible picture of the manna that fell in Israel's camp (Exod. 16:31).

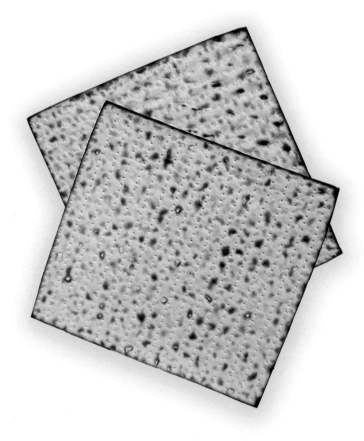

## MATZO BREAD

This Jewish Passover bread, called matzo, is a picture of the body of Christ. Notice the furrows (stripes), the brown surface (bruises), and the holes, an imagery of the nail prints on His hands and feet!

## BLOOD ON THE DOOR

At the first Passover in Egypt, the lamb's blood was applied to the left, right, and top door posts on the Hebrew homes. This was a picture of the future crucifixion of the "Lamb of God," Jesus Christ, and the three crosses on Golgotha.

## QUMRAN COMMUNITY

The remains of the Qumran community are near the Dead Sea. These men, called Essenes, copied the sacred scrolls and understood the communal meal and the banquet of the Messiah.

## GETHSEMANE

The old olive trees in the Garden of Gethsemane are a reminder of the night when Christ became sin with our sins and sick with our sicknesses (Matt. 8:17).

# GIANTS

The race of giants and the brother of Goliath, Lahmi (1 Chron. 20:5), are a reminder of how the enemy will attempt to bring back what God has removed from your life, including sickness.

## PRAYER SHAWL—TALLIT

In Matthew 9:20, when the woman touched the hem of Christ's garment, it was the blue thread (fringes) of His prayer shawl (tallit). The blue thread represented heaven and was a reminder of God's covenant.

## THE SHOWBREAD

Just as fresh bread was placed on the table of showbread in the temple, believers need fresh manna, including the Communion meal of the bread and cup of the Lord.

## THE DIDACHE AND THE COMMUNION MEAL

One of the oldest manuscripts that describes some of the earliest Christian teachings is called the Didache. The manuscript, which was discovered in 1873, was translated in 1883. Scholars fix the date of the writing at about A.D. 100 to 120, which is about the same time that the last book of the New Testament, Revelation, was compiled by the apostle John. It is not just another parchment or book that someone compiled, but was actually considered part of the early church's instructional guidelines.

The Didache contains several important concepts that were taught in the first century. The first part of the manuscript describes the "two paths of life and death," which deals with Christian behavior and morality in life. For example, it is written, "Do not abort a fetus or kill a child that is born." It instructs to pray the Lord's Prayer three times a day. It also admonishes believers to fast twice a week, on Wednesdays and Fridays. One interesting instruction deals with baptism in water:

> Now concerning baptism, baptize as follows: after you have reviewed all these things, baptize in the name of the Father and of the Son and of the Holy Spirit in running water. But if you have no running water, then baptize in some other water; and if you are not able to baptize in cold water, then do so in warm. But if you have neither, then pour water on the head three times in the name of the Father and Son and Holy Spirit.
>
> —DIDACHE 7:1–3

The Communion meal is also discussed in the Didache:

> On the Lord's own day gather together and break bread and give thanks, having first confessed your sins so that your sacrifice may be pure. But let no one who has a quarrel with a companion join until they have been reconciled.
>
> —DIDACHE 14:1–2

This is the same admonition given by Christ, that a believer should not attempt to offer a gift at the altar until they are first reconciled to their brother (Matt. 5:23–24). Christ also taught that if a believer did not forgive his brother's trespasses, the one holding the grudge against his brother could not be forgiven himself (Matt. 6:14–15).

According to the Didache, the following prayers were offered, first over the fruit of the vine and then the bread:

> We give you thanks, our Father, for the holy wine of David your servant, which you have made known to us through Jesus, your servant; to you be the glory forever.
>
> —DIDACHE 9:2

> We give thanks, our Father, for the life and knowledge which you have made known to us through Jesus, your servant; to you be glory forever. Just as this broken bread was scattered upon the mountains and then was gathered together and became one, so may your church be gathered together from the ends of the earth into your kingdom; for yours is the glory and the power through Jesus Christ forever.
>
> —DIDACHE 9:3–4

A third prayer was prayed after the conclusion of the meal:

> To us you have graciously given spiritual food and drink, and eternal life through your servant.... Gather your church from the four winds into your kingdom, which you have prepared for it: for yours is the power and glory forever. May grace come, and may this world pass away. Hosanna to the God of David. If anyone is holy, come; if anyone is not, let him repent. Maranatha! Amen!
>
> —DIDACHE 10:5, 9–14

Several points should be made here. First, notice that David, not Abraham, is mentioned in two of the three prayers. This may be because the promise of the Messiah was through the lineage of David. Abraham was promised the land of

Israel, but David was promised the kingdom of the world to come. Since the Communion meal looks forward to the future kingdom, then David as the heir to the future kingdom would be mentioned in the Communion prayers.

Second, in two of the three prayers there is a request to gather the church from the four winds. This theme of the gathering of the church was revealed by the apostle Paul in 1 Thessalonians 4:16–17 and Ephesians 1:9–10. It is the moment when the dead in Christ will be raised and the living saints will be changed from mortal to immortal. Together, they will be caught up to meet the Lord in the air! Paul calls these events the "gathering together unto him [Christ]" in 2 Thessalonians 2:1.

At the Last Supper, Christ said He would not eat or drink again until He did so in the kingdom. Christ reminded His disciples of drinking the cup in the future kingdom and that our receiving Communion is a continual reminder of the return of the King, the resurrection of the dead, the catching away of the saints, and the gathering together at the great banquet supper in the heavenly city.

The third interesting observation is the third prayer and the word *Maranatha*. The same word is found in 1 Corinthians 16:22, where Paul closed his letter by saying, "If any man love not the Lord Jesus Christ, let him be Anathema [meaning cursed or separated]." Paul then says, "Maranatha." This is an Aramaic word meaning "our Lord comes." Because the word is an Aramaic word and not a Hebrew or Greek word, some suggest that it was invented by the early Christians as a code word to identify the real believers in times of persecution.

## THE THREE MEALS OF THE SABBATH

Even today among the religious Jews, the Sabbath is a very important day. God established six days in which to work and the seventh day as a time of rest (Gen. 2:2). Paul taught that there remains an eternal rest (Sabbath) for God's people, which we will enter the moment Christ returns (Heb. 4:1–11) At that time, we will participate in our "Sabbath meal," as alluded to in Revelation 19:7.

According to Jewish mystical commentaries, there are three meals on the Sabbath day:

Therefore one must wholeheartedly rejoice in these meals, and complete their number (three altogether), for they are meals of the perfect Faith, the Faith of the holy seed of Israel, their supernal Faith, which is not that of the heathen nations.

—ZOHAR 2, PAGES 88 A–B

The third meal was identified in early Judaism as the "holy meal of the Ancient One," or the "meal of the King." It is also called by Jewish sages, "the Meal of the Messiah." This third meal is also called "escorting the queen," which describes the festivities that conclude the Jewish Sabbath.

An example of this third meal may be alluded to in Acts 20. Paul was ministering in Troas for seven days, and at the conclusion of his time (the Sabbath), he preached until midnight. As the oil lamps were burning late at night, a young man named Eutychus, who was sitting on a window ledge, fell to the ground three stories below. The fall killed the fellow, but Paul prayed for him and he was raised up. Paul went back to the upper room where he broke bread and ate. Paul continued to speak to the believers until daybreak (Acts 20:7–12).

After this late night (third) meal, Paul was still ministering! This was a normal activity after the third meal was eaten. The final discussion at the third meal often points to the return of the Messiah and the coming kingdom. Therefore, the third Sabbath meal is a special meal identifying the Meal of the Messiah.

## THE LORD'S TABLE AND RECONCILIATION

Paul refers to the Communion as the "Lord's table" (1 Cor. 10:21). Paul may have been comparing this with the table of showbread in the temple. This golden table contained twelve pieces of holy bread, one for each of the twelve tribes of Israel. Each week the priests were permitted to eat the twelve loaves from this table. At the same time, another set of priests would bake fresh bread to replace the eaten bread, and the following week that bread was eaten and replaced again.

The idea of the Lord's Table is linked to the bread used in the Communion. Christ said that He was the bread come down from heaven, and He instructed us to eat His flesh and drink His blood in order to have life. This can refer only to the Communion meal, or the meal that heals!

After the destruction of the Jewish temple in A.D. 70, the Jews wrote that, "As long as the Temple stood, the altar at the Temple atoned for Israel, but now a man's table atones for him" (Talmud, Berakhoth 55a). The temple stood in Christ's time, and He and His disciples often ascended to the holy house for prayer (Mark 11:11; Acts 3:1). Gifts and offerings were a part of the daily routine. Christ made it clear that for God to bless any gift, it must be given with a pure heart not tainted by strife and unforgiveness.

This was the emphasis of the apostle Paul when he said we should examine ourselves when we are sitting with our brothers and sisters at the Lord's Table.

> But let a man examine himself, and so let him eat of that bread, and drink of that cup.
> —1 CORINTHIANS 11:28

This self-examination is for the purpose of looking inwardly to examine one's relationship with God and man. Since the brass altar no longer exists in the temple in Jerusalem, the Lord's Table becomes the altar of examination. I must continually emphasize that before receiving the bread and the cup, one should repent to God and then repent and make reconciliation to their fellow believers.

Communion is a reminder of what Christ has done, a reminder of what He can do now (heal and continually deliver), and a reminder of the world to come.

> Let us be glad and rejoice, and give honour to him: for the marriage of the Lamb is come, and his wife hath made herself ready. And to her was granted that she should be arrayed in fine linen, clean and white: for the fine linen is the righteousness of saints. And he saith unto me, Write, Blessed are they which are called unto the marriage supper of the Lamb. And he saith unto me, These are the true sayings of God.
> —REVELATION 19:7–9

## THE CLIMAX OF THE COMMUNION MEAL

At the Last Supper the Lamb of God, the future Priest of the heavenly temple, raised the silver chalice and announced that He would not drink it again until the future kingdom arrived. At that great heavenly banquet, when the white-robed saints assemble in the largest banquet hall ever known, the Messiah—the Bridegroom—will once again lift the silver cup in the air, and we will once and for all seal the marriage of the bride and the Groom!

### FOR YOUR REFLECTION

1. Describe how the Communion meal may have been first observed by the Essenes.

   _____

   _____

   _____

2. What admonition does the Didache give concerning the observance of the Communion meal?

   _____

   _____

   _____

3. Christ referred to "the meal that heals," or Communion, when He described Himself as "the bread come down from heaven," and instructed us to eat His flesh and drink His blood in order to have life. The apostle Paul instructs believers to "let a man examine himself, and so let him eat of that bread, and drink of that cup" (1 Cor. 11:28). What is the purpose of this self-examination before partaking of Communion?

_____

_____

_____

4. What event will signal the climax of the Communion meal as we
   know it?

_____

_____

_____

# CHAPTER 12

# HOW TO RECEIVE THE COMMUNION MEAL

But let a man examine himself, and so let him eat of that bread, and drink of that cup.

—1 CORINTHIANS 11:28

WALKING WITH GOD IN the new covenant should keep our vertical relationship with God in line with the Word, and our horizontal relationship with men in line with God's Word. When a vertical line and horizontal line intersect, they form a cross. All of mankind's redemption, deliverance, and healing form at the cross of Christ.

When receiving the Communion meal that represents the blood and body of Christ, I believe there is an important four-part process that we should initiate before we receive the meal and then follow at the conclusion of the meal.

## LOOK INWARD

Prior to receiving Communion, believers should look inward into their hearts and spirits. This inward self-examination is to ensure that we have no hidden or known sin in our lives. The Bible says, "But let a man examine himself." The Greek word for *examine* means, "to reach a result from an inquiry."[1] A self-examination is like placing an MRI or a spiritual X-ray into your mind and spirit. After all, it is what comes out of a man's mouth (from his heart) that defiles a person (Mark 7:18–23).

If your heart senses a feeling of guilt, then immediately repent and ask God for forgiveness and cleansing. This action will keep you humble before God as well as pure in mind and spirit. As a result, you will live a healthier and fuller life.

## Look Outward

After looking inward, then look outward. Has strife, misunderstanding, or disagreement created a rift between you and a family member, friend, or fellow believer? Discern your relationship with others around you. Life is not perfect, and at times people will disagree. The Bible teaches that, if we have an aught against a fellow believer, our gift (offerings) will not be blessed until we first go to our brother or sister in Christ and make restitution (amends):

> Therefore if thou bring thy gift to the altar, and there rememberest that thy brother hath aught against thee; leave there thy gift before the altar, and go thy way; first be reconciled to thy brother; and then come and offer thy gift.
> —Matthew 5:23–24

Restitution, or reconciliation, is the theme of the new covenant. If Christ forgave us, then we should forgive others.

## Look Upward

As believers eat the bread and drink from the cup, they should meditate upon the finished redemptive work of Christ, recognizing that He suffered on our behalf and that through His death and resurrection we can enjoy a threefold atonement. We can be made whole in our spirit, soul, and body. As we look upward to our High Priest, Jesus Christ, we should meditate upon the goodness of God and His mercy toward us.

## Look Onward

Live every day with the expectance that you will fulfill your God-given assignments and live out all of your days. Seize the promise of Psalm 91:16: "With long life will I satisfy him, and shew him my salvation."

One of the great faith ministers was Smith Wigglesworth. In his earlier days, Smith was healed, and he emphasized the healing gifts during his long ministry. Even in his time, he received the revelation of daily Communion. Smith lived to be eighty-seven years of age and passed away quietly while in a church service. This is the way to go! Live out your assigned days, and, when you are ready to go, fall asleep on Earth and wake up in heaven!

## SEVEN IMPORTANT CONSIDERATIONS FOR COMMUNION

Let's discuss the actual procedure for the communion service.

### The location

The location can be anywhere in your home where you can spend a few moments of quality time with the Lord. I have a home office, and at other times I receive Communion at a small table in our kitchen area. It is important to have an atmosphere and time in which there is not a lot of noise or distraction. After all, you are approaching the High Priest in the heavenly temple!

### The bread

I suggest you purchase a box of Jewish Passover bread, called matzo bread, from a local store. If this is not possible, then use unsalted crackers. If you can purchase some that were made without leaven, this is the best. However, if this is not possible, then use bread that is available. Remember that once the bread is blessed, God recognizes what you are doing.

### The fruit of the vine

I personally believe it is best to use pure grape juice. This can be purchased in any local grocery store. Many prefer the red grape juice as a picture of the blood of Christ. Again, it is when the juice is blessed that it becomes more than simply grape juice.

### The cup

While any cup can be used, I prefer to have a special silver cup set aside just for the Communion meal. Silver cups can be purchased at various stores. Keep the cup in a special place, and use it just for the Communion meal. Jewish sources can provide these cups for purchase. Our ministry also has a portable kit that can be purchased while they are available.

### The time to receive

In the time of the tabernacle and temples, a lamb was offered in the morning and in the evening (Exod. 29:38–39). These were called the morning and evening sacrifices. The morning is typically when a person begins the activities or the work of the day, while evening is when he or she prepares to rest at night. The altar of the Lord had lamb's blood sprinkled in the morning and in the evening. I believe it is best to receive Communion in the morning, before we begin our day and become too busy. Also, what we entertain on our mind the first thing in the morning often sets the pattern for the entire day.

### The prayer

Below is an example of a prayer that you can pray. As you grow in the grace and knowledge of God, pray a simple prayer from your heart.

*Heavenly Father, I thank You for sending Your Son, Jesus Christ, to redeem mankind. I thank You that, through Christ's sufferings, He purchased a threefold redemption for my spirit, mind, and body. Today I ask You to bless this bread that represents the body of Christ. Bless the fruit of the vine that represents His precious blood.*

*Father, as You have forgiven me, so I forgive those who have sinned against me. Lord, I forgive and release anyone who has wronged me, and I ask You to search my spirit and remove any trace of sin or disobedience from my life. Today, I release from my mental prison anyone who has hurt me in any way, and I ask You to bless them and help them spiritually.*

*Father, as I receive this Communion, I ask You to bring strength and health to me spiritually, emotionally, and physically because of the new covenant that was sealed through the sufferings of Christ. Jesus carried my infirmities; therefore, I ask You to lift from me what Jesus has carried for me.*

*I receive it by faith, and I give You all the glory and honor, in the name of Jesus Christ. Amen.*

If you are receiving Communion first thing in the morning, clear your mind and heart of all distractions and fully concentrate upon the wonderful graces of God. Pour the fruit of the vine into the cup, take a piece of bread in your hand, and, with your own words of prayer, bless the bread and the cup. Thank God for sending Christ to redeem you.

If you are in need of healing, begin to quote the promise, "With the stripes of Jesus I am healed." In prayer, tell the Lord that you believe the blood of Christ was shed for your atonement, including your physical healing. Believe, as you receive Communion, that the life of Christ is working in your body, driving out every sickness, disease, and weakness that is hindering your life.

Remember that this is not a magical formula, but a sacred moment between you and your heavenly Father. If a person does not receive Communion every day, they should do so at least once a week. Do not allow this act to become a religious ritual where you lose the meaning.

### The time of worship

It is good to spend a few moments in worship after receiving Communion. Perhaps you enjoy singing a song to the Lord. During a Jewish Passover, there are special psalms that are designated to be sung. The Bible tells us that, after the Last Supper, Christ and the disciples sang a hymn:

> But I say unto you, I will not drink henceforth of this fruit of the vine, until that day when I drink it new with you in my Father's kingdom. And when they had sung an hymn, they went out into the mount of Olives.
>
> —MATTHEW 26:29–30

Because this was the Passover season, Christ would have sung hymns from the Psalms, such as, "This is the day the LORD has made; we will rejoice and be glad in it" (Ps. 118:24, NKJV). To sing from your heart to the Lord, you do not need musical accompaniment or the church choir. Paul wrote:

And be not drunk with wine, wherein is excess; but be filled with the Spirit; speaking to yourselves in psalms and hymns and spiritual songs, singing and making melody in your heart to the Lord.

—EPHESIANS 5:18–19

The Old Testament psalms, which were originally songs, are still used as songs today among the religious Jews. Spiritual songs are birthed by the Holy Spirit as you are in His presence. These are songs that come forth from your own spirit when worshiping in God's presence.

While encouraging you to worship, I am reminded of the woman from Lebanon who asked Christ to heal her sick daughter. Christ let her know that she was a Gentile and that He was sent to minister to those in Israel. She then began to worship (Matt. 15:21–28). Christ cannot ignore a person's sincere worship. He was moved with compassion and sent His word and healed the daughter. She was made whole that very hour (v. 28).

This simple process can become a part of your daily life's routine, and it can create an important window of time for you to spend with the Lord. It can also be a great physical, mental, and spiritual blessing to you.

## CONCLUDING THOUGHTS

After many years of full-time ministry, I have discovered an important key to receiving from the Lord. All truth must be processed through the intellect, where we reason and weigh the evidence that we receive:

Come now, and let us reason together, saith the LORD.

—ISAIAH 1:18

For spiritual truth to impact your life, it must be quickened to your inner spirit. As the psalmist once said:

Remember the word unto thy servant, upon which thou hast caused me to hope. This is my comfort in my affliction: for thy word hath quickened me.

—PSALM 119:49–50

The word *quickened* means "to make alive." There are times when you hear a message from God's Word and you are intellectually motivated. At other times, you are uplifted and blessed. There are occasions when the Word of God pierces into your soul like a sword and discerns your thoughts and the intents of your heart (Heb. 4:12). Then there are those times when the message you are hearing or the book you are reading seems to come alive in your spirit. You know when this happens because the information becomes revelation as the eyes of your understanding are opened (Eph. 1:18). The truth seems to jump from the pages, and suddenly you can sense inwardly a strong witness that God will move on your behalf.

The spiritual truth you have read must become more than a book in your hands for this message to impact your life. It must quicken your heart and spirit. When the written or spoken Word of God becomes alive and energized in your heart, that is called a *rhema* word. The word *rhema* is one of the Greek words translated in the New Testament as "Word of God." Two examples where the word *rhema* is translated as Word of God are:

> So then faith cometh be hearing, and hearing by the word [*rhema*] of God.
> —ROMANS 10:17

> And take the helmet of salvation, and the sword of the Spirit, which is the word [*rhema*] of God.
> —EPHESIANS 6:17

Once the Word of God moves from intellectual reasoning to a quickened, living word in your spirit, then faith will enter your spirit! You are able to believe what God has spoken and respond to His Word in faith. This has personally happened to me on several occasions. I recall praying for several months for direction in my ministry. During a special service in Ohio, the Holy Spirit quickened my spirit to act on my faith and, in obedience, the Lord would meet the needs of our ministry. I acted in faith, and He met the needs.

I want to emphasize again that the concept of Communion is biblical and should be practiced whether or not a person is physically sick. If you attend a church where

Communion is offered, then by all means receive the Blessed Sacrament. Examine your relationship with God and with man, and repent before both if necessary.

In Judaism, a distinction is made between sins committed against God and sins committed against a fellow man. This is clear from the Old Testament sacrifices. One offering was known as a sin offering, and another was marked as a guilt offering. The sin offering was a sacrifice made when one sinned against the Word of God. However, the guilt offering was made as a form of restitution when a person sinned against a fellow man. The guilty person not only went before God for forgiveness, but he also went before the person against whom he had sinned. This is why Jesus said:

> Therefore if thou bring thy gift to the altar, and there rememberest that thy brother hath aught against thee; leave there thy gift before the altar, and go thy way; first be reconciled to thy brother, and then come and offer thy gift.
>
> —MATTHEW 5:23–24

Just as Jesus would say, "Again I say unto you" (Matt. 19:24), I wish to remind you that one of the greatest roadblocks to healing is unforgiveness and strife. You will never receive your complete healing if you allow strife and contention to rule your life. Both my father and I have seen people receive wonderful answers to prayer after they began confessing their faults and forgiving those who have mistreated them (James 5:16).

In conclusion, I am emphasizing inner cleansing through repentance because I do not want to see this powerful covenant of healing through the Lord's Supper become null and void due to a hidden sin or attitude that is not confessed and forsaken. I also wish to say again that this is not magic, nor is it medicine. Each person must judge this teaching in his or her own spirit and act accordingly. Whether we receive Communion daily, weekly, or monthly, we must do it in a spirit of understanding and faith. None of us have a guarantee of life tomorrow. But I believe it is biblical that we can live out our appointed days and then depart in peace. *The Meal That Heals* gives you the biblical revelation that God has established to help you do just that.

## FOR YOUR REFLECTION

1.  What is the purpose of each of the following steps to be taken during the period of self-examination before a Communion meal?

    a.  Look inward

    _____

    _____

    b.  Look outward

    _____

    _____

    c.  Look upward

    _____

    _____

    d.  Look onward

    _____

    _____

2.  Give a brief description of each of the following procedural steps for taking Communion:

    a.  The location

    _____

    _____

    b.  The bread

    _____

    _____

    c.   The fruit of the vine

_____

_____

    d.   The cup

_____

_____

    e.   The time to receive

_____

_____

    f.   The prayer

_____

_____

    g.   The time of worship

_____

_____

3.   What biblical revelation have you received from reading this book that will help you to establish a practice of receiving Communion regularly?

_____

_____

_____

# CHAPTER 13

# ANSWERING YOUR QUESTIONS
# ABOUT DAILY COMMUNION

*If any of you lack wisdom, let him ask of God, that giveth to all men liberally, and upbraideth not; and it shall be given him.*

—JAMES 1:5

**Question:** *Can I force someone to receive Communion if they do not believe it has the power to bring healing? Will the Lord still heal someone who does not believe it is possible to be healed by God's power?*

**Answer:** Some Christians understand only the salvation component found in the Atonement and do not believe in any form of healing, especially physical healing. All blessings in the new covenant operate through faith. Salvation is received by faith. Deliverance is received by faith. The Holy Spirit baptism is received by faith. Healing is also received by faith. Every promise in the new covenant is released through a person's faith in that promise. The Bible says:

> For indeed the gospel was preached to us as well as to them; but the word which they heard did not profit them, not being mixed with faith in those who heard it. For we who have believed do enter that rest…
>
> —HEBREWS 4:2–3, NKJV

The Word must be mixed with faith. In Nazareth, Christ could not do mighty miracles because of their unbelief (Matt. 13:58). In answer to your question, we cannot force a person to accept Christ, we cannot force them to be baptized in water, and we cannot force them to receive the baptism of the Holy Spirit. Faith involves the free will of each person. Therefore you cannot force a person to receive Communion, and really, you shouldn't—lest they receive it unworthily.

**Question:** *My pastor told me that only an ordained minister is permitted to perform the Lord's Supper and told me the teaching of daily Communion was not biblical.*

**Answer:** I believe we have proven from Scripture and history that not only is it biblical, but it was also common in the first century; however, it was later lost through the traditions of men. In a local church assembly, it is true that the minister (a pastor or a priest) overseeing that assembly should perform the service. However, keep in mind that the true believers make up a kingdom of priests, and our bodies are now the temples of the Holy Spirit. Our homes are miniature sanctuaries where the Lord's presence dwells. Therefore, Communion in our home is a part of our intimate time with Christ.

**Question:** *I gave Communion to my seventy-five-year old father, and yet he passed away. What went wrong?*

**Answer:** Your father was seventy-five years of age, and, according to Scripture, we are told that we can live to be seventy and by reason of our strength, eighty. We are not limited to just eighty years, but we can live a full and complete life, seeing our children and our grandchildren. However, at some point we must all pass from this life and meet the Lord. Therefore, even the Communion supper cannot keep a person living endlessly or prevent death from finally taking us home. For example, the prophet Elisha received a double portion of the anointing of Elijah, yet he later fell sick and died (2 Kings 13:14). If a person has done all they know to do in order to be healed, but the person still passes away, we must trust the Lord that this was His time for that person.

**Question:** *I have noticed that some of the more traditional churches use real wine, with alcohol in the Communion, while others use grape juice. Why is this, and should it really matter?*

**Answer:** Part of the reason for the difference is the belief of the churches related to the use of alcohol. Many of the traditional churches have used fermented wine for centuries. However, most of the full-gospel and Pentecostal denominations use pure grape juice. In part, this is because of their teaching that a believer should abstain from the use of alcohol in any form.

When Jesus held up the cup and introduced the new covenant, He called the cup the "fruit of the vine." As stated earlier, according to Jewish historical sources, when wine was used at the Passover, a cup was mixed with three parts water and one part wine to ensure that any alcohol level would be reduced to the point of having no impact on the person drinking the wine.

Jesus Christ was sinless. In the Bible, normal bread contains leaven, and wine that sits for long times becomes fermented. In Scripture, leaven represents sin. The bread at Passover and at Communion has no leaven because Christ was without sin. Fermentation occurs in wine when the juice begins to break down and bacteria sets in. Fermented wine has gone through this decaying process. Because the fruit of the vine is a picture of the blood of Christ, and Christ's blood was pure and untainted by the sin nature of Adam, I believe that it is preferable to use pure grape juice. I believe the juice is a better representation of the pure, sinless blood of Christ.

**Question:** *What type of bread should be used during Communion? I see some churches that use a small round wafer; others, crackers; and some use pieces of bread. Is there a certain type of bread that should be preferred over others?*

**Answer:** For convenience, a local congregation will often use grape juice and a wafer that is pre-packaged. Others use a large wafer, and some offer pieces of bread. One point should be made. Whatever bread or wafer is used should not have leaven in it, since leaven represents sin and Christ was a perfect, sinless sacrifice.

For Passover, the Jewish people use a special bread called matzo bread that is baked. As stated previously, the matzo bread is a perfect picture of sufferings that affected the physical body of Christ. This bread can be purchased in many of the major food chains in the United States. I keep a box of this bread at home and in my office.

If you are unable to obtain this bread, then use what is available and bless the bread prior to receiving it. In your prayer, speak to the Lord and tell Him you are recognizing this bread as the precious body of the Lord. God certainly understands each situation and the limitations believers may experience. For example, in an Islamic nation, you cannot find the Jewish bread, but you can find other types of bread, or a person can bake their own bread without leaven and set it aside for the Communion meal. Remember, it is your faith and the sincerity of your heart that God honors.

---

**Question:** *I am a prisoner and cannot get grape juice for Communion, and it is impossible to get the Jewish bread. However, I want to receive Communion. Will the Lord still honor my faith even though I am unable to obtain the juice and the bread?*

**Answer:** Your question reminds me of a comment in the Didache as it relates to water baptism. It states that if a believer cannot baptize in water, then pour water over the head three times, in the name of the Father, Son, and Holy Spirit. This was written for a person who was unable to get out of their home or who may live where there was no water for baptism (such as in a barren desert or a remote mountain region). I once had two individuals on our Holy Land tour who, for medical reasons, could not get into the cold water to be baptized. I quoted the Didache, which was used in the early church, and poured water over them using the above formula. They both cried, and we rejoiced together.

The point is that there may be an older person who cannot get out of their home, so there was an option available based on extenuating circumstances. In prison you cannot get the items required for Communion. If Jesus can take water and turn it into wine, then a prisoner may need to use simple water and a piece of bread. Again, it is the intent of the heart that moves God.

**Question:** *Don't you believe that if a person receives Communion too often, it will become too commonplace and soon lose its effect?*

**Answer:** This is a concern that I have heard expressed by some. However, it is like saying if I read the Bible too often I will get tired of the Scriptures, or if I pray too much I might lose sight of the importance of prayer. A person who loves Christ will never fear that spending too much time with Him (including receiving Communion) will somehow cause one to become indifferent to it—at least not when they understand the power of intimacy with Christ through the bread and the cup.

**Question:** *How old should a person be before he or she is permitted to receive Communion?*

**Answer:** This can be answered by asking, "How old should a person be before he receives Christ as his personal Savior?" Children were attracted to Jesus, and He took time to spend with them and actually blessed them through His prayers. Each child matures at a different level. Some are more spiritually sensitive than others and tend to receive the gospel easier and accept Christ at a younger age.

Once a child can understand the simple plan of salvation and comprehend the purpose of Communion, I believe they are eligible to receive it. Both my son and daughter received Communion at about age five, in our home during the New Year. We made sure they had received Christ and understood Jesus's death, burial, and resurrection.

Some suggest (as does the Didache), that a person should be baptized in water before receiving the Lord's Supper, since water baptism is the public sign that a person has received Christ as his Savior.

**Question:** *Should a person receive Communion if he knows for certain he is living a life of hidden sin? Is this receiving it unworthily?*

**Answer:** I recall as a young child when my father pastored local churches, he would announce that the congregation would be receiving the Lord's Supper the next Sunday. It was amazing how many members did not show up. Some would say, "Well, preacher, I might not be living where I should be, so I'm not going to take the Lord's Supper and be unworthy and have trouble come to me."

I never understood their way of thinking. If they felt unfit to receive Communion because of some sin, then why not get the sin out of their life and receive Communion? They were correct in judging themselves, but they condemned themselves by their own self-examination. The purpose of self-evaluation is to look inward and remove the sin so your heart will be right with the Lord. It appeared to me they missed the point and definitely missed the blessing.

As human beings who are capable of sinning, none of us are worthy in ourselves to receive the favor and grace of the Lord. It is because of the precious blood of Jesus that we are made worthy to receive any blessings from the Lord.

---

**Question:** *When do you personally receive Communion? Is there a set time of the day, week, or month?*

**Answer:** I especially receive Communion when I am sensing a spiritual warfare, when I feel that I need more intimate time with God, or if I am encountering a physical attack against my body. Sometimes I receive it at the office and sometimes at home. My wife and I also receive it at the local church we attend. I would suggest to those who have a sickness or disease that they receive Communion every day if possible.

If you go to a doctor and the doctor prescribes a prescription and instructs you to take the medication every morning for the next year because it will help you, you will take the written prescription to a local pharmacy, purchase the medicine, and take the prescription according to the instructions of the doctor. If you are encountering physical difficulty, I believe this is where receiving daily Communion is important. Do it in the same manner that you would when a doctor prescribes medicine.

**Question:** *If I am sick and believing that the Lord will heal my body, will it happen instantly or gradually? How will I know I am healed? How can I confirm it?*

**Answer:** It can happen instantly or gradually. I tell people not to quit taking any medication from a doctor unless the physician tells them that they are now free from the illness or they no longer need the medication. Most people will know when the healing has occurred because the symptoms of the disease will disappear, or the healing is confirmed by a medical checkup.

When Christ healed certain individuals, He instructed them to go to the temple and show themselves to the priest. In Christ's time, the priests were instructed and well informed on how to determine if a person (such as a leper) had been cured of his disease. Once the persons were pronounced healed, they returned home to their family and were permitted back into public life.

At times you will know you have been healed. However, medical tests are sometimes needed to confirm that the healing has occurred. It is not a lack of faith to be tested by a medical doctor to prove there a positive change in your situation.

**Question:** *My family thinks that receiving Communion at home is some type of a new religious cult that is arising. They are very traditional. How can I convince them otherwise?*

**Answer:** If they will read this book with an open mind and carefully examine the detailed information, I believe it will help them understand the concept. Remember, whenever a truth that had been ignored or suppressed from the past was resurrected in the church, the truth was received by some and rejected by others. Eventually, as the message was spread and taught, the eyes of men and women were opened, and they received the truth and were blessed by the revelation.

A person cannot force another person to believe and accept any truth from Scripture. We can, however, walk in the light and live the life, demonstrating that the truth works.

## FOR YOUR REFLECTION

1. What additional questions do you have regarding the covenant of Communion?

_____

_____

_____

2. How will you attempt to have your questions answered?

_____

_____

_____

# CHAPTER 14

# WHY SHOULD YOU DIE
# BEFORE YOUR TIME?

Do not be overly wicked, nor be foolish: Why should you die before your time?
—ECCLESIASTES 7:17, NKJV

ONE OF GOD'S HEBREW names, Jehovah Rapha, indicates God's plan for healing His people. Throughout both the Old Testament and the New Testament, healing was provided, and through the stripes of Christ we can be healed. With such evidence of God's willingness and ability to heal the sick, why are so many Christians not wading out into the refreshing streams of God's healing covenant? Why are some believers passing away before fulfilling the scriptural promise of a long life? This has been a perplexing question, even among full-gospel theologians.

In two parts, I will attempt to provide some answers to this perplexing question. The first part will deal with the reasons why some godly believers may encounter a premature death, and the second section will cover the subject of the greatest hindrance to receiving your healing.

We all understand that death is a fact of life. If Christ does not return in our lifetime, we will all enter death's door. It should, however, be our goal to live as long as we can. In Scripture we read where Joseph lived long enough to see his son Ephraim's children of the third generation (Gen. 50:23). Job lived to see his son, his sons' sons, and even four generations (Job 42:16). Proverbs 3:2 reveals, "For length of days, and long life, and peace, shall they add to thee." Yet, some people, even some good Christians, die from accidents, crime, or disease. Solomon made an interesting statement when he said, "Do not be overly wicked, nor be foolish: Why should you die before your time?" (Eccles. 7:17, NKJV).

It is possible for a person to die a premature death. Paraphrasing Solomon's statement, "Don't get involved in wickedness or do foolish things that could cause you to die early." We know that alcohol, illegal drugs, overeating, eating wrong foods, or engaging in dangerous actions can all place a dead-end-ahead sign on the road of life. Many teens have cut short their appointed time by engaging in foolish behavior or by being with the wrong crowd at the wrong place at the wrong time. We have all known of someone who lived a pure, godly life and died from a terrible disease or in a sudden accident. When we ponder why someone's life was shortened, many questions arise that are difficult to answer.

## THE PRE-FLOOD GENERATIONS

God intended men to live long, enjoyable lives. This is clear when examining the genealogical names of the first ten righteous men in the Bible. Moses recorded their names and revealed how long each man lived. Prior to the Flood, the first ten generations of righteous men, from Adam to Noah, lived very long lives.

- ✦ Adam lived 930 years (Gen. 5:5).
- ✦ Seth lived 912 years (Gen. 5:8).
- ✦ Enos lived 905 years (Gen. 5:11).
- ✦ Cainan lived 910 years (Gen. 5:14).
- ✦ Mahalaleel lived 895 years (Gen. 5:17).
- ✦ Jared lived 962 years (Gen. 5:20)
- ✦ Enoch lived 365 years (Gen. 5:23).
- ✦ Methuselah lived 969 years (Gen. 5:27).
- ✦ Lamech lived 777 years (Gen. 5:31).
- ✦ Noah lived 950 years (Gen. 9:29).

There are numerous theories regarding the secret to their lengthy life span. Some suggest there was a special canopy covering the earth that was destroyed during the

Flood. Others believe the underground water that men drank was energized, thus rejuvenating the cells of the bloodstream and renewing the body.

Others suggest that continual sin and wickedness of mankind resulted in God reducing the number of years of mankind's life. The Flood was initiated by God because of man's wickedness, violence, and evil imaginations (Gen. 6:11–13). Pre-Flood men lived to be hundreds of years old. What if men today lived that long? A righteous man could impart righteous teaching to generations of people. A wicked man such as Adolf Hitler could use his additional years to create weapons of mass destruction and spread his hatred of the Jews until the Jewish people would be completely destroyed. After the Flood, there was a significant reduction in the number of years that people lived.

## THE POST-FLOOD GENERATION

Following the worldwide flood, the next ten generations experienced a reduction in the number of years they lived. Death came to them much sooner than it had their previous ancestors. Here is what the record shows:

+ Shem lived 600 years (Gen. 11:10–11).
+ Arphaxad lived 438 years (Gen. 11:12–13).
+ Salah lived 433 years (Gen. 11:14–15).
+ Eber lived 464 years (Gen. 11:16–17).
+ Peleg lived 239 years (Gen. 11:18–19).
+ Reu lived 239 years (Gen. 11:20–21).
+ Serug lived 230 years (Gen. 11:22–23).
+ Nahor lived 148 years (Gen. 11:24–25).
+ Terah lived 205 years (Gen. 11:32).
+ Abraham lived 175 years (Gen. 25:7).

The total number of years of the first ten generations is over eight thousand years. The combined number of years the next generation is slightly over three thousand years. This pattern of reducing man's time on Earth continued with the next ten generations, beginning with Abraham's descendants. Abraham's son

Isaac lived 180 years (Gen. 35:28). Joseph, the son of Jacob, lived 110 years (Gen. 50:26). After Joseph, the Bible ceases to list the age of the sons of Jacob when they died in Egypt. We do know that many years later, Moses passed away at age 120 (Deut. 34:7). Scripture reveals God's final promise of how long a man could live:

> The days of our lives are seventy years; and if by reason of strength they are eighty years, yet their boast is only labor and sorrow; for it is soon cut off, and we fly away.
>
> —Psalm 90:10, NKJV

In summary, the Bible records that, from Adam to Noah, men lived up to 969 years. After the Flood, man's life span was reduced from 600 years (Noah) to 175 years (Abraham). Hundreds of years after Abraham, Moses died at age 120 (Deut. 34:7). Moses wrote that man's days are now 70 years, and if we have strength, our lives can extend up to 80 years. Some live beyond 80 years, since 80 is not a final number, but a number given in general terms. Living at least 80 years enables the average person to have children, see their grandchildren, and even their great-grandchildren.

## THE PROMISES OF LONG LIFE

The Word of God has given believers several promises of a long and fulfilling life.

> With long life I will satisfy him, and show him My salvation.
>
> —Psalm 91:16, NKJV

> For length of days and long life and peace, they will add to you.
>
> —Proverbs 3:2, NKJV

> Hear, O my son, and receive my sayings; and the years of thy life will be many.
>
> —Proverbs 4:10

The fear of the LORD is the beginning of wisdom: and the knowledge of the holy is understanding. For by me thy days shall be multiplied, and the years of thy life shall be increased.

—PROVERBS 9:10–11

## WHY SOME NEVER FULFILL THESE PROMISES

Even with these wonderful Scriptures of long life, we all have known of good Christians who never fulfill these promises. Sometimes this is because the unexpected occurred; for example, a young couple had been married, and, soon after, the bride was suddenly struck with a terminal disease that took her life. Or a group of miners were suddenly killed while working in a coal mine. Perhaps a child is taken in a tragic and unexpected accident. In some cases, missionaries who were working for God's kingdom were killed by the very people they were attempting to reach.

Through the years, some of the leading ministers in the body of Christ have experienced the heartache of seeing their own children die through an accident. I know of five world-recognized ministers whose children died in accidents. None died from a disease or a sickness, but through plane or car accidents, work-related tragedies, a car jacking, and a gang shooting. These tragedies create questions in the minds of family and close friends, such as, "Why would God allow the child of a man or woman of God to be taken at such an early age?" Is there an answer to this question?

## AN AMAZING VISITATION

Several years ago a dear friend, Pastor Walter Hallam from LaMarque, Texas, experienced a heartbreaking tragedy when his beautiful seventeen-year-old daughter was taken from this earth through a plane accident. Walter shared that he had great sorrow in his heart and that he had many questions concerning her death. As with any parent, he felt it was unjust that God had allowed his daughter, an anointed teenager who served as a youth pastor and operated in the gifts of the Spirit, to be taken at this early age. After forty days of great sorrow and questions, the Lord appeared to Walter early one morning in his bedroom and began to share with him one of the most astonishing revelations he had ever heard. It helped to answer several questions that were on his heart.*

Walter had reminded the Lord it was unjust that his daughter had been taken. The first thing Christ told him was that three of His own great men were taken by tragic circumstances and that too was not just. Christ reminded Walter that both James and John the Baptist were beheaded and Stephen was stoned. Christ said, "It was not just." As Christ continued a detailed discourse with Walter, He expounded on four stories recorded in Luke chapter 13. Using these stories, Christ revealed four reasons why some people die.

The first story was found in Luke 13:1–2:

> There were present at that season some that told him of the Galilaeans, whose blood Pilate had mingled with their sacrifices. And Jesus answering said unto them, Suppose ye that these Galilaeans were sinners above all the Galilaeans, because they suffered such things?

In history, while some Galileans were making a sacrifice, Pilate gave orders to have them killed. Josephus taught that the Galileans were wicked and open to fighting. However, Jesus asked the people of His day, "Were they worse sinners than other sinners?" The answer was no. They did not die because they were sinners. They died because of Pilate. Jesus revealed to Walter that some people die because of cults and false religions. For example, radical followers of Islam have beheaded some Christians for their faith. Some believers have been burned to death by radical Hindus. False religions and cults have taken the lives of young people throughout the world.

The second story from Luke 13 that Christ related was as follows:

> Of those eighteen, upon whom the tower in Siloam fell, and slew them, think ye that they were sinners above all men that dwelt in Jerusalem?
>
> —LUKE 13:4

---

* I want to thank Pastor Walter Hallam of Abundant Life Christian Center, LaMarque, Texas, for permission to share this story. Pastor Hallam can be contacted via e-mail: pastor@alcc.org.

In history, the pool of Siloam was located south of the temple in Jerusalem. It is where the blind man in John 9:7 was healed. In the story (and in history), it appears that a large, stone guard tower that was built near the pool suddenly collapsed and killed eighteen innocent people who were simply being refreshed at the cool waters of this famous pool.

Using this example, Jesus told Walter, "There are some people who die because of accidents, or by chance, because we live in a fallen realm. Ever since Adam and Eve sinned in the Garden of Eden the curse has been in operation in the earth. Because we now live in a cursed or fallen world, accidents can happen." At that point the Lord talked to Pastor Hallam about the term *by chance*. It means "inadvertently or by accident."

Christ revealed a third reason:

> He spake also this parable; A certain man had a fig tree planted in his vineyard; and he came and sought fruit thereon, and found none. Then said he unto the dresser of his vineyard, Behold, these three years I come seeking fruit on this fig tree, and find none: cut it down; why cumbereth it the ground? And he answering said unto him, Lord, let it alone this year also, till I shall dig about it, and dung it: And if it bear fruit, well: and if not, then after that thou shalt cut it down.
>
> —LUKE 13:6–9

In this Scripture passage, Jesus emphasized bearing fruit and the importance of being diligent to do your work. Because the servant had failed to dig and till the ground, as was his job, the tree had no production; therefore, it was removed. At this point the Lord reminded Pastor Hallam of scriptures in the Books of Proverbs and Psalms about diligence in work. He then said to Pastor Hallam, "When men fail to do their work correctly, it often opens the door for the curse and for accidents to come." The point was that some people who are not bearing fruit can open the spiritual door to events that can lead to death or accidents.

As an example, years ago one of my spiritual converts was eating lunch with my family. After the meal, he drove his car down the hill and crashed into the guardrail. Flipping in the air, he was thrown out of his van and died in intensive care two days later. The brakes on his van had failed. He knew that the brakes were bad, but he never took the time to fix them. If the brakes had worked, he might still be with us.

As Christ pointed out that morning, if a person does not do his job properly, it can cause an accident. Some are taken because their brakes were not fixed, the plane was not serviced properly, the electric wiring was faulty, or someone ran a red light. God did not cause the accident; it was human failure that created the circumstances.

The fourth reason why some die was revealed in Luke 13:11:

> And, behold, there was a woman which had a spirit of infirmity eighteen years, and was bowed together, and could in no wise lift up herself.

This Jewish woman was a daughter of Abraham, and she was bound by a spirit of infirmity. Some sickness is simply because of disease, illness, bad diet, health laws, and so on, but some sickness is because of a spirit of infirmity. A spirit of infirmity (this word means weakness) had caused a physical sickness for eighteen years. Of course, Christ liberated the woman, and she was totally cured. Jesus pointed out to Pastor Hallam that some people die of illnesses that are caused by spirits of sickness and infirmity. If a sickness that is caused by a spirit is not dealt with, then the person could pass away before his or her appointed time.

When Pastor Hallam shared this powerful visitation from Christ with me, I was greatly moved. It was the greatest explanation I had ever heard as to why some die earlier than others. It was the only explanation I had heard that made rational and spiritual sense, because it was a word from the Lord Himself. Though there may be many other reasons why people die prematurely, these are the four the Lord pointed out to Pastor Hallam when talking to him about accidents and tragedies that can occur.

We all must acknowledge that there are times when someone, including a wonderful believer in Christ, passes on and there is no explanation for it. We must realize there are some things that will remain a mystery to us unless God Himself reveals the reason to us. On the other hand, we should believe God for a long life and take whatever measures necessary to fulfill our days.

After years of observing tragedies in the life of believers, I believe there are three keys that, in many cases, can help prevent tragedies from occurring.

### 1. Be sensitive to the circumstances around you.

I have known of pilots who overruled their better judgment and flew in terrible storms that resulted in a plane crash. Other people ignored the danger and drove through flooded roads, only to be swept away by the current. Taking a shortcut through the rough side of town can have a tragic ending. We should not live in fear, but we should be sensitive to our circumstances and surroundings and use good judgment. Doing so will help us avoid a wrong decision that could lead to difficulties or loss of life.

### 2. Follow a burden in your spirit.

When you sense a burden or a weight in your spirit, it is often a signal that change is coming. It can also be a warning nudge that a difficult time of trouble is ahead. My father is a great prayer warrior who taught me that when I feel an inner burden, it is a signal to pray or intercede on someone's behalf. On three occasions, my father felt a strong sense of danger, and in all three instances, our family was involved in car accidents. Nobody was killed, and in two accidents we walked away from our vehicle without a scratch. Advance prayer had formed an invisible hedge.

When you feel a burden in your spirit, get alone and pray until you receive a release from the heaviness you are experiencing. This relief is a signal that your prayer has been heard and God is moving on your behalf.

### 3. Be sensitive to the inner nudges of the Holy Spirit.

Years ago a Christian coal miner was praying before going to work. He was strongly impressed of the Holy Spirit not go to work that morning. A few hours later, the local mine exploded, killing all of the miners. Years ago my father was traveling alone to Ohio to visit his family. He stopped at a rest stop and noticed a lone van in the parking lot. Dad felt a strong inner nudge of the Holy Spirit not to go into the men's room, but to get back in the car and leave. As he did, three rough-looking men opened the van door and ran toward his car. Dad managed to quickly drive away.

No doubt their intention was to harm Dad, but through his obedience to the Holy Spirit, God spared him from danger. Had he not been spiritually in tune, no doubt he would have been harmed.

## HOW DOES COMMUNION FIT IN?

Clearly we live in a world dominated by Satan and his evil agents (Eph. 2:2; 6:12). At times we are subject to circumstances that create difficulties and danger. While Communion cannot prevent an accident, stop a criminal, or prevent an unexpected tragedy, the quality time that we spend with God during Communion can sharpen our spirits to be sensitive to danger and warnings and can help us fulfill our days.

## FOR YOUR REFLECTION

1. Prior to the Flood, humans often lived more than nine hundred years. After the Flood, the life span of humans continually decreased. What are some of the theories for this declining life span for humanity?

   _____

   _____

   _____

2. In Psalm 90:10, we read God's final promise to man about the length of his days. Write this verse on the lines below:

   _____

   _____

   _____

3. Through a miraculous revelation from God to Pastor Walter Hallam, who lost a seventeen-year-old daughter due to a plane accident,

Hallam was given four reasons why people may die prematurely and not be given long life as the Bible promises. Briefly describe each of these reasons:

a. Luke 13:1–2

_____

_____

b. Luke 13:4

_____

_____

c. Luke 13:6–9

_____

_____

d. Luke 13:11

_____

_____

4. What three keys does this chapter give that can prevent tragedies from occurring?

a. _____

_____

b. _____

_____

c. _____

_____

# CHAPTER 15

# SEVEN COVENANTS THAT BRING BLESSINGS TO YOUR LIFE

But now hath he obtained a more excellent ministry, by how much also he is the mediator of a better covenant, which was established upon better promises.

—HEBREWS 8:6

THROUGH OUR RELATIONSHIP WITH Jesus Christ, we have entered into a new covenant. Many Christians view their relationship with God as a sinner saved by grace battling the devil on the road to heaven, knowing that if they can hold on and endure the test and trials, they will make it. As a teenager, this is how I viewed my relationship with Christ—that is, until age eighteen when I came across a small booklet on the subject of our covenant with God. The information in that booklet changed my understanding.

I discovered that I was in covenant with God, just as Abraham and God had entered a covenant (Gen. 15:18). In a covenant relationship, people exchange their names, their possessions, and their power. God changed Abram's name to Abraham, began to bless him with possessions, and demonstrated His power throughout Abraham's life. A covenant relationship is what my wife and I entered when we exchanged marriage vows. My wife, Pam Taylor, exchanged her name

Taylor for my name Stone. All I owned became hers, and all she owned became mine. In the marriage vow we said, "For better or for worse, for rich or for poor, in sickness and in health." It was a commitment to stay glued to each other in good and bad times. Our marriage is based on unconditional love one for another. We do not demand anything from each other, but seek to make one another happy and keep the covenant bond firm.

All biblical covenants have certain conditions placed upon the promises. In the Abrahamic covenant, God required that the fathers circumcise their Jewish sons in the foreskin of their flesh eight days after their birth (Gen. 17:12). This fleshly circumcision was a token (sign) of the child's relationship with God through the Abrahamic covenant. If a Jewish man was not circumcised, then he would be cut off from among the people:

> And the uncircumcised man child whose flesh of his foreskin is not circumcised, that soul shall be cut off from his people; he hath broken my covenant.
>
> —GENESIS 17:14

In the time of Moses, God brought the Hebrew nation out of Egyptian bondage. He did so based upon a promise given to in Genesis 15:13. Once free, within weeks, the Hebrews built a golden calf and angered God. The Lord was prepared to destroy the entire nation and raise a righteous seed through Moses:

> And the LORD said unto Moses, I have seen this people, and, behold, it is a stiff necked people: Now therefore let me alone, that my wrath may wax hot against them, and that I may consume them: and I will make of thee a great nation.
>
> —EXODUS 32:9–10

Although these were God's covenant people, He was willing to destroy them, not because they were not circumcised, but because they were worshiping an idol. When the Hebrews crossed the line and willfully disobeyed God, the Almighty was under no obligation to honor the promises of His covenant. The blessings of the covenant are always based upon the condition of obedience. It is these conditions that inspire us to follow the Word of God.

## THE "IF" FACTOR

The word *if* is used 1,541 times in the King James Version of the Bible. The word can mean, "in the event that, granting that, or on the condition that." There are three areas where the word *if* is used that are significant:

+ The "if" of Satan
+ The "if" of man
+ The "if" of God

### The "if" of Satan

During the temptation of Jesus, Satan used the "if" twice. In each instance he was attempting to create unbelief in Christ's mind concerning His relationship to God. Satan was demanding that Jesus prove He was the Son of God:

> If thou be the Son of God, command that these stones be made bread.
>
> —MATTHEW 4:3

> If thou be the Son of God, cast thyself down.
>
> —MATTHEW 4:6

The "if" of Satan is designed to cause you to question the Word of God. When things are falling apart, people often have thoughts such as, "If God loves me, why is this happening to me?" Or, "If God answers prayer, why is my answer delayed?" Some question why they are not healed or why family members are not yet converted. When the adversary brings an "if" into your mind, it will always be to plant a seed of doubt toward the promises of God's goodness and His faithfulness.

### The "if" of man

A diseased leper who came to Christ took a great risk when he did so. Leprosy was considered contagious, and Jewish law said a leper had to stand one hundred to three hundred paces away from a clean person, depending upon the direction of the wind. On this occasion, the leper fell at Jesus's feet and said, "If thou wilt, thou canst make me clean" (Luke 5:12). In response, Jesus removed the "if" and said, "I will: be thou clean" (v. 13). Jesus removed the "if" of doubt, and the leper was immediately made whole!

The "if" of man is connected to knowing the will of God. Satan's "if" attempts to make a person doubt the *promises* of God, but the human "if" begins to doubt the *willingness* of God to perform what He has spoken. It does little good to believe that God can if you do not believe that God will. Think for a moment. God *can* save the lost, but *will* God save your family? God *can* baptize believers in the Holy Spirit, but *will* God baptize you in the Holy Spirit? God *can* heal, but *will* God heal you? The "if" of man questions the willingness of God to perform His promises.

### The "if" of God

The "if" of God, on the other hand, is a question about your willingness to be obedient to God's requests. While Satan plants doubt concerning God's promises and the human mind questions God's willingness, God's "if" is based upon your obedience. At times an "if" plays an important role in receiving a promise from God; for example, the Lord promised:

> If my people, which are called by my name, shall humble themselves, and pray, and seek my face, and turn from their wicked ways; then will I hear from heaven, and will forgive their sin, and will heal their land.
>
> —2 CHRONICLES 7:14

> If ye abide in me, and my words abide in you, ye shall ask what ye will, and it shall be done unto you.
>
> —JOHN 15:7

> If ye keep my commandments, ye shall abide in my love; even as I have kept my Father's commandments, and abide in his love.
>
> —JOHN 15:10

The "if" of God is always *a condition we meet* to receive the blessings promised us. If we do not humble ourselves and repent, then we cannot claim the promise of seeing our land healed. If we do not abide in Christ, then we cannot claim the promise of asking what we desire of Him. If we do not abide in the vine (Christ), then we cannot bear fruit.

The covenant we have with God contains promises and conditions.

+ Hearing the Word is the first condition.
+ Believing the Word is second condition.
+ Acting upon the Word is third condition.
+ Obedience to the Word is the final condition.

I have often wondered if the miraculous results in Christ's ministry would have been different if those needing miracles had not fully obeyed the Lord's instruction prior to the manifestation of the healing or deliverance.

If the disciples had asked for the little lad's lunch and said, "Jesus needs your lunch," what if the little fellow had replied, "If I give you my food, I won't have anything to eat!" What if the widow of Nain had told Jesus, "Don't interrupt my son's funeral; You know if You touch this coffin You will be unclean according to the law," would her son have been raised from the dead? When Jesus spit in the blind man's eyes and said, "Go wash," what if he had complained and said, "Are You crazy? I'm already blind, and now I've got mud stuck in my eye sockets!" Each miracle included an act of obedience. At times, it may seem foolish to the flesh and to some Christians when we act out our obedience and do what the Lord commands us to do. However, God loves and honors our obedience.

## YOUR PERSONAL COVENANT RELATIONSHIP

Your personal covenant relationship with Christ is the root of all spiritual, physical, emotional, and financial blessings that will flow from the heavenly storehouse into your life. This covenant requires you to follow the scriptural instructions in the New Testament. Understanding how Satan, your human mind, and God use the word *if* is important to claiming the benefits that have been promised. Again:

- The "if" of Satan questions the *Word* of God.
- The "if" of man questions the *will* of God.
- The "if" of God is a condition of your *obedience*.

It is important to understand the "if" factor because God's "if" is a condition, and any covenant comes with certain conditions attached. Every covenant has three elements:

1. Promises: what you will receive from the covenant
2. Agreements: what is expected from you out of the covenant
3. Conditions: what you must do in order to receive full benefit from the covenant

Just as marriage is a covenant with these three aspects, so your walk with God is a covenant with the same three important concepts.

### 1. Promises

On their wedding day, a couple repeats a series of vows to publicly affirm their lifelong commitment to one another. These vows are made before a minister, before people, and before God.

Both the Old and New Testament covenants consist of promises. God promises to release His blessings and His gifts to those who will enter into covenant with Him. As Scripture says, "The promises of God in him are yea, and in him Amen" (2 Cor. 1:20).

### 2. Agreements

After the vows are repeated, the minister says, "Do you...," and the man and woman respond with the words, "I do." Those are strong English words to affirm an agreement. Once the couple agrees to the promises, then the marriage covenant is legally sealed in the eyes of God and the witnesses.

In the Bible, God gave the revelation of the covenants, including the blessings and the promises granted for obedience. In Abraham's covenant, the fathers agreed to circumcise their sons as a sign of the covenant. In return, God promised to bring forth a mighty nation and prosper Abraham's descendants in all they set their hands to do.

### 3. Conditions

While love should be unconditional, the marriage vows come with spiritual conditions. The condition is *faithfulness* to your marriage partner. When a partner becomes unfaithful by committing adultery, then the marriage vows are broken. Some marriages have been restored through humility and repentance, but often the act of adultery causes the spouse to be crushed in spirit, which leads to separation and divorce.

This was the case with Israel when God brought the nation out of Egyptian bondage. Days later, while Moses was interceding and receiving the law of God, the Hebrews were dancing before a golden calf. God's anger was kindled, and He threatened to destroy Israel and raise a new nation through Moses. Only through intercession was Israel spared (Exod. 32:8–35). After years of Israel rebelling against God, the Lord finally said He was divorcing Israel:

> And I saw, when for all the causes whereby backsliding Israel committed adultery I had put her away, and given her a bill of divorce; yet her treacherous sister Judah feared not, but went and played the harlot also.
>
> —JEREMIAH 3:8

In the new covenant, we are commanded to abide in the Lord and remain faithful to Him and His Word (John 15:4–10). As we grow in the Lord, we will experience blessings in every area of our lives.

## THE COVENANT BLESSINGS

Our covenant with Christ impacts three areas mentioned in 1 Thessalonians 5:23:

> And the very God of peace sanctify you *wholly*; and I pray God your whole *spirit* and *soul* and *body* be preserved blameless unto the coming of our Lord Jesus Christ.
>
> —EMPHASIS ADDED

Three New Testament words identify the area where God's wholeness occurs:

1. Justification: This is a spiritual act where God delivers the spirit from the penalty of sin.
2. Sanctification: This is a spiritual act where God delivers the soul from the power of sin.
3. Glorification: This is the final stage at the resurrection where we are free from the presence of sin.

Between the time of our salvation (when we are justified) and our entry into heaven (when we are glorified) we must walk in the power of the Spirit and live by the regulations and promises of the new covenant.

## THE SEVEN COVENANTS

There are seven covenants that God ordained that are designed to be a blessing for your life.

### 1. The salvation covenant

This is the most important covenant in Scripture. Without this covenant you will not have eternal life. This covenant is entered into when you ask Christ to forgive you of your sins and you accept Him as your Lord and Savior. Paul wrote:

> For with the heart man believeth unto righteousness; and with the mouth confession is made unto salvation.
>                                                             —ROMANS 10:10

This covenant defeats sin, which is inherent in all people. Every person has the potential to sin. When a person yields to sin, the punishment ends in death. However, the power of the blood of Christ overcomes the power of sin and death when a person repents of their sins and receives Jesus Christ as his or her personal Savior.

### 2. The healing covenant

Another covenant is the healing covenant. Adam and Eve's disobedience in the Garden of Eden produced a set of twins called sin and death. At the cross

Christ brought a double cure for the double curse. He defeated sin and death and arose from the grave with the authority over death, hell, and the grave (Rev. 1:18).

There was no sickness until after the fall of mankind. Physical infirmity is linked to the fall of Adam and the natural aging process. Christ provided more than victory over sin; He sealed a covenant of healing through bearing in His body the sickness of mankind. As Peter wrote:

> Who his own self bare our sins in his own body on the tree, that we, being dead to sins, should live unto righteousness: by whose stripes ye were healed.
>
> —1 Peter 2:24

Christ's beaten body sealed the healing covenant, and His shed blood sealed the salvation covenant. When we receive the body and the blood of Christ, we signify that we have entered into the salvation covenant and believe that Christ's healing covenant will manifest in our physical bodies.

### 3. The Holy Spirit covenant

When Jesus ascended to heaven, He told His disciples that He would send another comforter to abide with them forever (John 14:16). The word *Comforter* is *parakletos*, which means, "one who intercedes for, one who counsels or comforts."[1] Jesus is our intercessor in heaven, and the Holy Spirit is our intercessor on earth. The Holy Spirit was a promise to those who were in covenant with Christ. This gift of the Holy Spirit (Acts 2:18) is exclusively for the children of God (Luke 11:13). He provides a prayer language for each believer to communicate directly to the Lord (1 Cor. 14:2). Christ has promised the Holy Spirit as a blessing for your obedience to the covenant.

### 4. The marriage covenant

Marriage is between a man and a woman. A woman who is a virgin sheds a small amount of blood the moment she consummates with her husband. This was so important in the Old Testament that the following morning the sheets from the bed were presented to the elders of the city. If the woman was not a virgin, she was stoned (Deut. 22:14–21).

This shedding of blood demonstrates that marriage was intended to be a blood covenant between one man and one woman, for life. Marriage is a wonderful covenant and a great blessing when a person finds their life mate.

### 5. The church covenant

> For by one Spirit are we all baptized into one body, whether we be Jews or Gentiles, whether we be bond or free; and have been all made to drink into one Spirit.
>
> —1 CORINTHIANS 12:13

It may seem unusual to say this, but God ordained the church, Christ predicted the birth of the church, and He gave Himself for the church (Matt. 16:18; Acts 20:28). The church is not one particular denomination, but it consists of all believers who have a salvation covenant with Christ. The Greek word for "church" is *ekklesia*, which means, "a calling out for a meeting."[2] The church represents the "called-out ones" who have been called to receive Christ.

While every believer is part of the universal church of Jesus Christ, it is important to find a local congregation and become involved with the local believers. Remember, Christ addressed seven major churches in the Book of Revelation, and the church is His body. Paul taught that men are to love their wives even as Christ loved the church (Eph. 5:25). We must respect and love the church because it is the virgin that is espoused to Christ (2 Cor. 11:2). *SON OF GOD*

### 6. The family covenant

God loves a family. In the beginning of Creation, angels were called sons of God (Job 38:7). After the fall of Lucifer from heaven, God created Adam, and he was called a son of God (Luke 3:38).

Following Adam's expulsion from Eden, God arranged a covenant with Abraham and brought forth Israel, whom he called, "My son" (Exod. 4:22, NKJV). When Israel began to break the covenant, God then sent His only begotten Son,

Jesus Christ, who did not sin; neither did He fail to fulfill His Father's assignment. Christ then produced a spiritual family, and now we are called the sons of God (1 John 3:2).

God desired a family. He has a spiritual family from all nations, kindred, tongues, and people (Rev. 7:9). God understands the joy of having a spiritual son or daughter, watching them grow and mature, and hearing them say, "Father, I love You!"

God has given men and women on Earth the ability to procreate and birth a family. In a time when children are rejected in the womb, abandoned by their parents, and abused by adults, God's Word still says, "Lo, children are an heritage of the LORD: and the fruit of the womb is his reward" (Ps. 127:3). One reason God selected Abraham as His covenant man to birth the nation of Israel is written in Genesis:

> For I know him, that he will command his children and his household after him, and they shall keep the way of the LORD, to do justice and judgment; that the LORD may bring upon Abraham that which he hath spoken of him.
> —GENESIS 18:19

God saw that Abraham would teach his children and pass the covenant on from generation to generation. After all, God's blessings are generational!

## 7. The financial covenant

The seventh covenant God established is a financial covenant. It is God's will for His people to prosper in all they set their hands to do. Prosperity is established in both the first and second covenants:

> But thou shalt remember the LORD thy God: for it is he that giveth thee power to get wealth, that he may establish his covenant which he sware unto thy fathers, as it is this day.
> —DEUTERONOMY 8:18

> Beloved, I wish above all things that thou mayest prosper and be in health, even as thy soul prospereth.
> —3 JOHN 2

Out of these seven covenants, notice how many are connected to blood, or blood and water:

1   Salvation—because of the blood of Christ and the water of baptism.
2.  Healing—by the stripes (blood) of Christ.
3.  Holy Spirit—because of Christ death, resurrection, and ascension.
4.  Marriage—blood is shed when a virgin consummates her marriage.
5.  Church—become a member through the blood of Christ and water baptism.
6.  Family—a child is born in a mixture of water and blood.
7.  Finances—our offerings to God are compared to the sacrifices on the altar.

It is very clear that God loves covenants and loves to see His creation enter into covenant with Him.

## FOR YOUR REFLECTION

In this chapter the author describes the seven covenants that God ordained, which are designed to be a blessing in your life. On the lines under each covenant, describe how that covenant has already blessed your life. Then briefly describe the blessing that you are still awaiting for each covenant.

1.  The salvation covenant

    How God has already blessed me through this covenant:

    _____

    _____

    How I still am praying for God's blessing through this covenant:

    _____

    _____

    _____

2. The healing covenant

How God has already blessed me through this covenant:

_____

_____

How I still am praying for God's blessing through this covenant:

_____

_____

3. The Holy Spirit covenant

How God has already blessed me through this covenant:

_____

_____

How I still am praying for God's blessing through this covenant:

_____

_____

4. The marriage covenant

How God has already blessed me through this covenant:

_____

_____

How I still am praying for God's blessing through this covenant:

_____

_____

5.  The church covenant

    How God has already blessed me through this covenant:

    _____

    _____

    How I still am praying for God's blessing through this covenant:

    _____

    _____

6.  The family covenant

    How God has already blessed me through this covenant:

    _____

    _____

    How I still am praying for God's blessing through this covenant:

    _____

    _____

7.  The financial covenant

    How God has already blessed me through this covenant:

    _____

    _____

    How I still am praying for God's blessing through this covenant:

    _____

    _____

# CHAPTER 16

# BUILDING A FAMILY ALTAR IN YOUR HOME

And ye shall teach them your children, speaking of them when thou sittest in thine house, and when thou walkest by the way, when thou liest down, and when thou risest up.

—DEUTERONOMY 11:19

THE FIRST PASSOVER WAS in a home. Jewish Passover celebrations are today celebrated in the home. The first churches in the New Testament were in homes. Jews believe that your home is a miniature sanctuary, a place where God's presence should dwell. Even the doorposts of the homes are marked with God's Word with a small cylinder encased in a parchment, called a *mezuzah*. With such emphasis on the home, why should we not accept the concept that God would have us commune with Him through prayer, worship, Bible study, and the Lord's Supper in our homes?

Each family should have a special place in their house for a family altar. In early days, many saints would mark a special room of a section of the bedroom as their "prayer closet." From this special area the believer would read the Bible, commune with God in prayer, present petitions and prayer requests, and spend time in worship. Much of the believer's intercession centered on his or her family, especially the children or grandchildren.

In Scripture, men would build an altar as a memorial to remind each generation of God's covenant promises. Abraham, Isaac, and Jacob all three built altars and offered a sacrifice to God from the sacred stones of the altars (Gen. 22:9; 26:25; 33:20). When special needs arose, the patriarchs would return to the altar to remind God of His promises and covenant.

Even Christ spoke of having a special place where you can shut the door in secret and pray:

> But you, when you pray, go into your room, and when you have shut your door, pray to your Father who is in the secret place; and your Father who sees in secret will reward you openly.
>
> —MATTHEW 6:6, NKJV

An altar is a meeting place between a person and God. We are familiar with the altars in a church, but we can set apart any place in our home as our secret place with God.

1. *Set aside a place that is not in the flow of traffic.* In our home I have three places that can be used as an altar. The first is a personal office with doors that can be shut if I choose to pray. The second area is the living room, which is a wonderful place to pray late at night because it is quiet and peaceful. The third area is either the master bedroom or the guest bedroom. At times, to keep from disturbing the family, I will go into the guest room and close the door and pray. I like the idea of having several choices in case one area is not available or is too noisy.

2. *Have the proper study material in the room.* This includes Bibles, other books, and note pads. I keep notes so that I can later refer back to what I have written.

3. *Find a place where you can have the Lord's Supper.* In my office and at home, I keep grape juice and matzo bread.

4. *Pray over your family.* Both father and mother should pray over their children. Even if you are a single parent, use your spiritual authority to pray, instruct, and live by example.

## Healing Through the Blood of Christ

Most Christian churches accept the importance of salvation through the blood of Christ. Many, however, either do not accept or do not fully comprehend the second aspect of Christ's atoning work, and that is healing through the blood of Christ.

God established a healing covenant with ancient Israel in the wilderness. The Almighty announced that He was the Lord who healed them (Exod. 15:26). God established a covenant healing name, Jehovah Rapha, to identify Himself as a healer to His people.

Throughout the Old Testament, God performed amazing miracles for His chosen people. In the New Testament, healing of the body and soul was a central aspect of Christ's ministry, and the healing covenant continued in the early church. While some theologians relegate physical healing to a previous time and teach that healing is no longer possible in our contemporary time, the Bible totally contradicts this theological unbelief.

## The Prophecy of Isaiah

The prophet Isaiah, seven hundred years before Christ, predicted that the coming Messiah would not only redeem men but would also establish a healing covenant with the people. Scripture says:

> But He was wounded for our transgressions, He was bruised for our iniquities; the chastisement for our peace was upon Him, and by His stripes we are healed.
>
> —Isaiah 53:5, NKJV

God not only laid the sins of the world upon Christ, but He also placed the sickness of the world upon Him. Matthew spoke of this:

> When evening had come, they brought to Him many who were demon-possessed. And He cast out the spirits with a word, and healed all who were

sick, that it might be fulfilled which was spoken by Isaiah the prophet, saying: "He Himself took our infirmities and bore our sicknesses."

—MATTHEW 8:16–17, NKJV

I believe the sicknesses of humanity and the sins of the world were placed upon
Christ in the Garden of Gethsemane. This is why His stress level was so intense
that His sweat became blood. We know that prior to the crucifixion Christ was
beaten across His back with a cat-o'-nine-tails—a short-handled whip with nine
long leather straps embedded with glass or bits of metal. It was intended to rip the
victim's flesh apart. It would form rows of stripes and scar the back of the victim.

Why would the stripes on the back of Christ be the key to receiving healing for
our bodies? According to history, the Romans could beat a victim with an unlim-
ited number of strokes with the whip. The Mosaic Law allowed for up to forty
stripes to be given:

> Forty blows he may give him and no more, lest he should exceed this and
> beat him with many blows above these, and your brother be humiliated in
> your sight.
>
> —DEUTERONOMY 25:3, NKJV

In the Roman times it was common to whip the person with thirty-nine stripes.
Paul made this clear when writing about his own personal persecution he received
for preaching the gospel:

> From the Jews five times I received forty stripes minus one.
>
> —2 CORINTHIANS 11:24, NKJV

I once read where this developed from the belief that a person receiving over
thirty-nine stripes may die from the punishment and the purpose of the beating
was not to induce death but to induce punishment for a high crime. *Barnes Notes*
on the New Testament comments on this:

> In practice among the Hebrews, the number of blows inflicted was in fact
> limited to 39, lest by any accident in counting, the criminal should receive

more than the number prescribed in the Law. There was another reason still for limiting it to 39. They usually made use of a scourge with three thongs, and this was struck 13 times. That it was usual to inflict but 39 lashes is apparent from Josephus, Ant. 4. viii, section 21.[1]

*Adam Clarke's Commentary* gives details from the Jewish Mishna on how a beating was to occur:

> "The two hands of the criminal are bound to a post, and then the servant of the synagogue either pulls or tears off his clothes until he leaves his breast and shoulders bare. A stone or block is placed behind him on which the servant stands; he holds in his hands a scourge made of leather, divided into four tails. He who scourges lays one third on the criminal's breast, another third on his right shoulder, and another on his left. The man who receives the punishment is neither sitting nor standing, but all the while stooping; and the man smites with all his strength, with one hand." The severity of this punishment depends upon the nature of the scourge, and the strength of the executioner.[2]

Notice the three areas of the body where the stripes are borne:

1.  One-third on the left shoulder
2.  One-third on the right shoulder
3.  One-third on the breast

This mean Christ was struck thirteen times on the left shoulder, thirteen times on the right shoulder, and thirteen times on the breast. This is interesting because the blood of the lamb in Egypt was smeared in three locations on the doorpost—the left side, the right side, and the upper center mantle. The stripes were placed near the top of the body just as the blood in Egypt was on the upper parts of the door.

The number thirteen is also interesting in the Jewish faith. While thirteen is considered a number of bad luck in the West, it is a blessed number in the Jewish faith. Thirteen is the age in which a young man (or girl) enters adulthood. Religious Jews celebrate the bar mitzvah when a young man turns from twelve to thirteen years of age. He becomes the son of the covenant, and, at that point, he is responsible for his own personal sins. On the Feast of Tabernacles (which represents the future kingdom of the Messiah), thirteen bulls were offered. In the tabernacle and the temple, the bull offering was the sacrifice of consecration for the high priest and his sons (Exod. 29:9–10). The priests in Israel were given thirteen cities and their suburbs.

At the whipping post, Jesus bore the sicknesses of mankind. On His shoulders and upper back are stripes, and across His breast, the area of His heart, are wounds and stripes. These wounds and stripes are pictured in the matzo bread that is used in the Jewish Passover during the Passover seder. The bread is thin and baked without leaven. It has rows similar to stripes across the front and back of the bread. It is baked until the surface has a brown appearance. Before baking in the ovens, the moist dough is raked, and holes are pierced throughout the surface.

This is a perfect picture of the Messiah. Christ said He was the bread come down from heaven (John 6:41). We know that manna, the food that fell from heaven in the wilderness, is the food of angels (Ps. 78:25). Christ was the true bread from heaven. He had no leaven (sin), He was bruised and beaten with stripes, and the nails of the cross placed holes in His left hand, right hand, and both feet.

Christ's beating was for our healing. The cross was for our salvation. Adam's sin brought the duel curse of sin and sickness to mankind. Christ performed the double cure for the double curse!

## For Your Reflection

1. What steps have you taken to establish a family altar in your family?

_____

_____

_____

2.  What does this chapter reveal about the importance of the stripes Christ received before His crucifixion as it relates to healing?

    _____

    _____

    _____

3.  Briefly describe some of the interesting facts given in this chapter about the number thirteen.

    _____

    _____

    _____

4.  How are the stripes of Christ, which He received for our healing, symbolized in the matzo bread used in celebration of Passover?

    _____

    _____

    _____

# My Final Word to You

AFTER MINISTERING SEVERAL YEARS on the subject of daily Communion, I have been amazed and blessed by the many testimonies from men and women of all denominational backgrounds who received this truth in their spirits and acted upon it. Through the years, we have heard faith-building testimonies of how the Communion meal was a vital part of the person receiving a miraculous healing from a sickness or disease, or how it was the key in a spiritual recovery from an emotional attack of the enemy.

As I have previously indicated, Communion cannot keep a person alive forever in this life. Sooner or later we will die. Some depart by accidents, some through crimes of wicked men, and others by sickness or disease. I believe, however, that the Bible teaches we should not die before our appointed time, and we should desire to live out all of our days so we may have a fruitful and productive life.

The fact is, strong Christians who pray, read the Bible, attend church, tithe and give, and receive Communion are happier and know how to release stress better than those who see no importance in these activities. Communion really is a meal that heals!

## Chapter 1: God's Covenant of Healing for His Children

1.    Biblesoft, *New Exhaustive Strong's Numbers and Concordance with Expanded Greek-Hebrew Dictionary,* copyright © 1994, Biblesoft and International Bible Translators, Inc., s.v. *"sozo,"* NT:4982.

2.    Ibid., s.v. *"holos,"* NT:3650.

3.    Ibid., s.v., *"kanaph,"* OT:3671.

4.    Ibid., s.v., *"dunamis,"* NT:1411.

5.    Justin Martyr, *The Second Apology of Justin for the Christians Addressed to the Roman Senate,* "Names of God and of Christ, their meaning and power," Christian Classics Ethereal Library, http://www.ccel.org/ccel/schaff/anf01.viii.iii.vi.html (accessed May 28, 2008).

6.    Irenaeus, *Against Heresies: Book II,* "Further exposure of the wicked and blasphemous doctrines of the heretics," Christian Classics Ethereal Library, http://www.ccel.org/ccel/schaff/anf01.ix.iii.xxxiii.html (accessed May 28, 2008).

7.    Origen, *Contra Celsus, Book III,* chapter 24, NewAdvent.org, http://www.newadvent.org/fathers/04163.htm (accessed May 28, 2008).

8.    Clement, *Two Epistles on Virginity: First Epistle,* "Rules for Visits, Exorcisms, and How People Are to Assist the Sick, and to Walk in All Things Without Offence," NewAdvent.org, http://www.newadvent.org/fathers/0803.htm (accessed May 28, 2008).

9.    Theodore of Mopsueste, *Christlieb: Modern Doubt,* 321, in Adoniram Judson Gordon, *The Ministry of Healing* (Whitefish, MT: Kessinger Publishing, 2006), 62.

## CHAPTER 2: UNDERSTANDING THE COMMUNION MEAL

1.   Pliny the Younger, *Complete Letters*, "Gaius Pliny to the emperor Trajan, 96," trans. by P. G. Walsh (New York: Oxford University Press, 2006), 279.

2.   Cambridge Encyclopedia, vol. 52, s.v. "monstrance," http://encyclopedia .stateuniversity.com/pages/15360/monstrance.html (accessed May 29, 2008).

3.   Britannica Online Encyclopedia, s.v. "consubstantiation," http://www .britannica.com/EBchecked/topic/134483/consubstantiation (accessed May 29, 2008).

4.   John Charles Ryle, *Light From Old Times or Protestant Facts and Men (1890)* (Moscow, ID: Charles Nolan Publishers, 2000), 58–59.

5.   Biblesoft, *New Exhaustive Strong's Numbers and Concordance with Expanded Greek-Hebrew Dictionary,* s.v. *"koinonia,"* NT:2842.

6.   The Orthodox Union, "The Day of Atonement: The Temple Service on Yom Kippur," http://www.ou.org/chagim/yomkippur/ykavodah.htm (accessed May 29, 2008).

## CHAPTER 3: WHAT DOES IT MEAN TO BREAK BREAD?

1.   *Barnes' Notes*, electronic database, PC Study Bible V3.2F (www .biblesoft.com: BibleSoft, 1997), s.v. "Acts 2:42."

2.   *Adam Clarke's Commentary*, electronic database, PC Study Bible V3.2F (www.biblesoft.com: BibleSoft, 1996), s.v. "Acts 2:42."

3.   *Jamieson, Fausset, and Brown Commentary*, electronic database, PC Study Bible V3.2F (www.biblesoft.com: BibleSoft, 1997), s.v. "Acts 2:42."

4.   *Matthew Henry's Commentary on the Whole Bible*, new modern edition, electronic database. Copyright © 1991 by Hendrickson Publishers, Inc., s.v. "Acts 2:42–47."

5.   A. T. Robertson, *Word Pictures in the New Testament* (Nashville, TN: B&H Publishing Group, 2000).

6.   F. C. Cook, *The Bible Commentary* (Grand Rapids, MI: Baker Book House, 1981).

7.   Thomas Whitelaw, *The Preacher's Complete Homiletic Commentary on the Acts of the Apostles*, vol. 25 (Grand Rapids, MI: Baker Book House, 1996).

8.   J. R. Dummelow, ed., *A Commentary of the Holy Bible* (New York: Macmillan Publishing Co., 1973).

9.   John Peter Lange, *Lange's Commentary on the Holy Scriptures* (Grand Rapids, MI: Zondervan, 1960).

10.   Johann Jakob Herzog et al., *The New Schaff-Herzog Encyclopedia of Religious Knowledge* (New York: Funk and Wagnalls Company, 1910).

11.   Biblesoft, *New Exhaustive Strong's Numbers and Concordance with Expanded Greek-Hebrew Dictionary*, s.v. "*dokimazo*," NT:1381.

## CHAPTER 4: SECRETS IN THE GARDEN OF GETHSEMANE

1.   Biblesoft, *New Exhaustive Strong's Numbers and Concordance with Expanded Greek-Hebrew Dictionary*, s.v. "*agon*," NT:73.

## CHAPTER 5: THE MYSTERY OF THE MANNA

1.   Biblesoft, *New Exhaustive Strong's Numbers and Concordance with Expanded Greek-Hebrew Dictionary*, s.v. "*mah*," OT:4100.

2.   Ibid., s.v. "*kephowr*," OT:3713.

3.   Ibid, s.v. "*kaphar*," OT:3722.

4.   Justin Martyr, as quoted in "The Meal of the Messiah in Jewish Sources," lecture given in Budapest by Finnish dean and theologian Dr. Santala, http://www.kolumbus.fi/risto.santala/buda/budap4.pdf (accessed June 24, 2008). The *Commentary on the New Testament From the Talmud and Hebraica* has a paragraph on the mingling of the wine and water at the Seder (Henrickson Publishers, Inc., 1989).

5.   The Temple Institute, "Shavuoth," http://www.templeinstitute.org/shavuoth/flour.htm (accessed June 24, 2008).

6.    Charles John Ellicott, ed., *An Old Testament Commentary for English Readers* (London: Oxford University, 1882), 284.

CHAPTER 6: THE PRIESTHOOD OF THE BELIEVER

1.    Biblesoft, *New Exhaustive Strong's Numbers and Concordance with Expanded Greek-Hebrew Dictionary,* s.v. "*hagios*," NT:40.

2.    Charles George Herbermann et al., eds., *The Catholic Encyclopedia* (New York: Encyclopedia Press, 1913), 228, viewed at http://books.google.com/boos?id =MnYqAAAAMAAJ&printsec=titlepage#PPA228,M1 (accessed May 30, 2008).

3.    Anthony John Maas, *A Day in the Temple* (Boston, MA: Adamant Media Corp., 2006), 73–74, unabridged facsimile of edition published in 1892, viewed at http://books.google.com/books?id=L43HKrWiM4YC&pg=PA73&lp g=PA73&dq=repairing+wall+in+holy+of+holies+priest+in+box&source =web&ots=9bKMEmiobP&sig=kzwhfHT834UCynbO3jXGqHWThuQ&hl= en (accessed June 2, 2008).

4.    Alec Garrad, *The Splendor of the Temple* (Grand Rapids, MI: Kregel Publications, 2001), 70.

CHAPTER 7: THE GREATEST HINDRANCE TO RECEIVING HEALING

1.    Biblesoft, *New Exhaustive Strong's Numbers and Concordance with Expanded Greek-Hebrew Dictionary,* s.v. "*meno*," NT:3306.

2.    Ibid., s.v. "*zogreo*," NT:2221.

3.    Ibid., s.v. "*aphiemi*," NT:863.

4.    Ibid., s.v. "*skandalon*," NT:4625.

5.    Ibid., s.v. "*katesthio*," NT:2719.

CHAPTER 9: WHEN SICKNESS TRIES TO RETURN TO YOUR HOUSE

1.    As told to the author in 1979 by Leonard Davis, who was present in the meeting the night the woman was prayed for.

## CHAPTER 10: THE SECRET POWER OF THE BLOOD OF THE LAMB

1. Biblesoft, *New Exhaustive Strong's Numbers and Concordance with Expanded Greek-Hebrew Dictionary,* s.v. "*dam,*" OT:1818.

2. This number is an estimation of the amount of blood shed during Passover, found in Dr. Randy Caldwell's teaching on the tabernacle.

3. Dake's Annotated Bible, s.v. "Matthew 37:33," commentary b.

4. Jerome, The Principal Works of St. Jerome, "Letter XLVI. Paula and Eustochium to Marcella," Christian Classics Ethereal Library, http://www.ccel .org/ccel/schaff/npnF206.v.XLVI.htm (accessed June 24, 2008).

5. Biblesoft, *New Exhaustive Strong's Numbers and Concordance with Expanded Greek-Hebrew Dictionary,* s.v. "*sluwph,*" OT:7779.

## CHAPTER 11: THE DIDACHE AND THE MESSIANIC BANQUET

1. Kaufmann Kohler, "Therapeutae," JewishEncyclopedia.com, http://www .jewishencyclopedia.com/view.jsp?artid=185&letter=T (accessed June 3, 2008).

## CHAPTER 12: HOW TO RECEIVE THE COMMUNION MEAL

1. Biblesoft, *New Exhaustive Strong's Numbers and Concordance with Expanded Greek-Hebrew Dictionary,* s.v. "*dokimazo,*" NT:1381.

## CHAPTER 15: SEVEN COVENANTS THAT BRING BLESSING TO YOUR LIFE

1. Biblesoft, *New Exhaustive Strong's Numbers and Concordance with Expanded Greek-Hebrew Dictionary,* s.v. "*parakletos,*" NT:3875.

2. Ibid., s.v. "*ekklesia,*" NT:1577.

## CHAPTER 16: BUILDING A FAMILY ALTAR IN YOUR HOME

1. *Barnes' Notes,* s.v. "1 Corinthians 11:24."

2. *Adam Clarke's Commentary,* s.v. "1 Corinthians 11:24."

# FREE NEWSLETTERS
## TO HELP EMPOWER YOUR LIFE

## Why subscribe today?

☐ **DELIVERED DIRECTLY TO YOU.** All you have to do is open your inbox and read.

☐ **EXCLUSIVE CONTENT.** We cover the news overlooked by the mainstream press.

☐ **STAY CURRENT.** Find the latest court rulings, revivals, and cultural trends.

☐ **UPDATE OTHERS.** Easy to forward to friends and family with the click of your mouse.

**CHOOSE THE E-NEWSLETTER THAT INTERESTS YOU MOST:**

- Christian news
- Daily devotionals
- Spiritual empowerment
- And much, much more

SIGN UP AT: **http://freenewsletters.charismamag.com**

8178